COMPOUND MARKETING

HOW SMART ENTREPRENEURS USE ASSET-BUILDING MARKETING STRATEGIES FOR AN UNFAIR GROWTH ADVANTAGE.

DAN NORRIS

Published by Dan Norris
http://dannorris.me

The moral right of the author has been asserted.

ISBN: 978-1-64184-448-2 (Paperback)
ISBN: 978-1-64184-449-9 (eBook)

TABLE OF CONTENTS

Call to Action. 1

1998. 3
    Learning from the experts 3
    A chance meeting with a generous mentor 7
    Design matters 9
    A group who cared 10
    What's the story?. 11
    How much should you spend on marketing?. 16
    Building assets. 16
    Compounding assets 18
    Compound marketing. 18
    The 4 Compound Marketing Strategies. 19

Part 1. Brand 21
    Why you can't delegate branding. 23
    The way companies think about branding is changing 24
    Brands are stories. 25
    How to achieve great design on a budget. 26
        Put in the work 26
        Care about design 28
        The 3 commandments of good design. 29

The design problem scale 29
Don't get feedback. 32
Have a good design process 34
Don't get too carried away. 36
Look at what the experts do 38
Use your greatest assets 40
Prioritize visuals 41
Remember design is contextual 42
Let designers justify their work 43
Find great designers. 45
Avoid tempting brand killers 47

Part 2. Story. 49

64,000 years in seconds. 49
How to build storytelling into your business 52
Why won't they write about me? 53
Types of stories 55
Founding Stories. 59
Customer stories 64
Product stories. 71
Improving your story with a villain 74
A $24m Marketing Gift 75
How to tell your story. 79
Where to tell your story. 82
What if there is no story 84

Part 3. Community 87

Engaging a community. 90
Peel back the curtain 91
Have a meeting place. 91
Don't let everyone in, keep them small 96
Run competitions 96

Give them something exclusive 98

Think of them when you create content 99

Bend rules for community members 99

Promote community members 100

Be accessible 100

Give them an identity 101

Multiple communities. 102

Part 4. Content **105**

What is content marketing 105

How businesses should think about content marketing. 107

Embrace Transparency. 107

Creation without expectation of immediate reward. 108

Always give value. 109

Forget ROI 110

Are you not entertained? 110

Love your community. 112

Have a purpose 114

Experiment 115

Content marketing under the Compound Marketing model. .115

Website. 116

Social Media 117

Brand design. 118

Online groups. 118

Merch 119

Blog posts/articles 120

Podcast 121

Newsletter. 122

Competitions - external. 122

Competitions - internal. 122

Press 123

Sales activations. 123

Events/in-person 124

Video 125

Live. 126

Apps 126

Community-generated content 126

Conclusion. **129**

Justifying your marketing 129

How to measure Compound Marketing 134

The ultimate measure 135

Use your intuition. 135

Avoid vanity metrics 136

Engagement 137

Engage, don't target. 138

Patience over persistence 139

Don't let Compound Marketing go wrong 140

How much Compound Marketing is the right amount? 141

Scaling Compound Marketing 142

Invisible Compound Marketing 142

Does Compound Marketing scale? 145

A new kind of entrepreneur. **147**

CALL TO ACTION

There are no calls-to-action or upsells in this book. I run a business full-time, focus 100% on that, and write books as a hobby.

I don't sell my personal books outside of having them available on Amazon, and I no longer monetize my writing or personal brand in any way. I shut all of that down when I launched my latest business, including my paid downloadable products, online challenges, direct book sales, online membership, speaking gigs, etc.

That was about four years ago, and I still make less money as a wage through my business than I did at the time through my personal brand. But I believe that, in business, focus is important. I also believe in playing a patient, long game and building something unique and valuable over time, instead of focusing on one year's worth of cash.

I have nothing to ask of you in reading this book. You bought it; you should just be able to enjoy it. I hope you do.

1998

LEARNING FROM THE EXPERTS

Monday, 23 February, 1998, 10:40 a.m.

I walked from the bus stop to the top of the city near the gardens and through the impressive entrance of Queensland University of Technology (QUT). QUT had a reputation for being a great business school—the best in Brisbane, in fact—and after barely hitting the minimum high school score of 9 (25 is the worst, 1 is the best), I was beyond excited to scrape into a bachelor of business, majoring in marketing.

Walking through the entrance that day, my excitement gave way to fear. The vibe of university is very different from school. Everyone seems to intuitively know where they are going, and there's no one there to really tell you, much less make you go to class. I didn't like this. Being told what to do is easy, figuring it out yourself, not so much.

I was still 17 and a very young 17. Not knowing where to go, I sat on the seat by the huge fig tree in the middle of the roundabout and rolled up a cigarette. I nervously smoked it while I watched hundreds of people walking around in every direction, quickly and with purpose. "Shit," I thought, "this is going to be harder than I thought."

Eventually, I gathered up the courage to ask someone where Z Block was, and I found my way into my first lecture, Marketing 101.

I didn't really know what marketing was. We didn't do it at school; it just seemed like one of the more fun majors to choose in my degree. But I was willing(ish) to learn, so I listened in and read the textbooks. Marketing was about 4 Ps: Product, Price, Place, and Promotion. It was about having the right product, having a competitive price, and promoting it to the right people in the right place. *Easy, I should do okay at this.*

Then we learned about the microenvironment, synergy in organizations between knowledge and identity and resources, and macro environment things like culture, demographics, economics, etc. This was turning into much more bullshit than I could handle.

Predictably, I failed the subject with a 2 out of 7, changed majors, and didn't take another marketing subject at university. Marketing clearly wasn't for me.

Monday, 19 June, 2006, 08:55 a.m.

At 8:55 a.m., on the 19th of June, 2006, I nervously walked into the coffee shop in the Hilton hotel. Once again, the topic of the day was marketing, but a lot had changed since entering the QUT lecture hall eight years earlier.

After failing marketing, I'd changed to human resources so my 2/7 in marketing could count toward my degree.

In 2001, I graduated with a bachelor of business degree majoring in human resources. I'd found a graduate job in a local consultancy starting part-time and eventually was offered my first full-time job, a graduate HR/IR consultant at $27,000/year. I couldn't believe that much money was written on a contract for me. It's still one of the most exciting things that has ever happened to me.

In 2002, I moved onto a better paying role in a government-owned company, Queensland Rail, at $40,000, still in HR. Over the next few years, I worked my way through different parts of HR and found myself looking after online learning, which I liked a lot more than the traditional types of HR jobs. I was excited about the technology part. But if I'm honest, I was a little bit bored with working for a government corporation; I wanted something a bit more exciting.

I often thought back to a conversation I had with my university mate Gareth a few years prior. We had gone through university together and were in our last year. We walked back through the gates of QUT to the train station home, and he said, "What are you going to do after university?" I thought about it honestly and said, "I'm really not sure. I hope I can get a graduate job and then have a decent career in HR." I returned the question, "What are you going to do?" He said, "I'm going to be successful. I'll get a graduate job in HR. I'll move up the chain of command, and be an HR manager and HR director for major firms, and sooner rather than later, start my own consulting business." I said, "How do you know?" He said, "I just know."

When working at Queensland Rail, I thought about this conversation with Gareth because I always felt that if he was so confident of success, why shouldn't I be confident of success? At some point, I started thinking maybe people like me *are* the people who start their own businesses. Maybe I could be a successful business guy?

When we built online training programs, we hired external consultants to do the work, but as I got more involved in the projects, I wanted to build them myself. I started learning how to code in my spare time, learning Photoshop and Flash and JavaScript out of "Sams Teach Yourself" books. Queensland Rail even put me through a multimedia diploma, the perks of working for the government!

But as I thought more about my conversation with Gareth and looked more and more at how much I was paying for what I was getting through the consultants, I wondered what it would be like to *be* one of the consultants as opposed to hiring the consultants. I knew they were paid pretty well because it was my job to pay them!

I started reading business books and got excited about somehow starting my own business. Reading *Rich Dad Poor Dad*[1] on the walk to work one day in early 2006 sealed the deal. This was my new plan.

Once I knew this was what I wanted, all I cared about was being an entrepreneur. Everything I did was to get me toward this single goal. I read story after story of successful entrepreneurs who started with nothing, failed, and then broken out to reach amazing success. Why couldn't I be one of those people?

---

[1] https://www.amazon.com.au/Rich-Dad-Poor-Teach-Middle/dp/1612680194

So in June 2006, shortly after being promoted, I quit to start a business building online training courses and websites. I was 26, and I'd never built a public website before in my life.

So at 8:55 a.m. on the 19th of June, 2006, walking into the coffee shop, I was very nervous.

John was a consultant I'd worked with while I was at Queensland Rail. He was in his mid-fifties, surfed every day, and liked to work two days a week. He was somewhat of a thought leader in his field of leadership coaching, and he was also one of the only people I knew who had their own business. He wasn't a cheap consultant by any means, but he'd offered to mentor me for free. To this day, I can only assume the reason was generosity.

He was there when I arrived; I got the feeling he spent a lot of time in coffee shops. He knew everyone there and acted like the place was his office.

"So," John asked, "How are you going to market this business?"

"I don't know," I responded nervously, 'I guess I'm going to try to find one customer, then do a good job and get referrals."

"You need a marketing plan, but before that, you need a competitive advantage," he offered. "What is your competitive advantage? Why would someone choose you instead of someone else? Lots of people make websites?"

I couldn't answer this question, either. Why does someone choose anyone?

He probed further, "How much are you going to charge for websites?"

"Um, I have no idea, I guess slightly less than everyone else charges?"

"Where are you going to find your customers? How are you going to promote the business?"

I couldn't answer any of these questions, but I also didn't fully understand why they were important. I thought I would do one job, do a good job, get referrals, and eventually build up a reputation and a brand around what I do. Then I would become one of the entrepreneurial success stories I'd read about.

But once again, the expert was telling me I needed a structured marketing plan. I needed to get my pricing right; I needed to figure out the best ways to promote; I needed a product. I was back learning about the 4 Ps of marketing, but this time, my life depended on putting them into action.

I had a mortgage for a pretty expensive house, and I had walked away from a very good secure income.

I took it upon myself to try everything I could to figure out this marketing thing so I could make my goal of having my own business a reality.

I tried to implement the lessons from my university lecturer, and I tried to take John's advice and build out a marketing plan. I joined small business groups and forums and tried everything that was suggested. I put ads in the Yellow Pages. I bought sponsored blog posts in business forums to try to get small business customers, and I dove deep into SEO, building out networks of hundreds of sites with exact match domains. When Adwords came in, I spent up big on keywords. I tried guest posting, I tried responses on Q&A websites, I tried presenting at events, I ran ads in marketing magazines, I branded my cars, I got a nice office, I used links on the bottom of sites and specific strategies for getting more referrals from existing customers, I did email marketing, landing pages, adding my business to listing sites and more. Then I tried other dodgy things like paying for automated software for getting links on other websites, and apps that followed people on Twitter so they might follow me back. I spammed influencers, I bought links on influential sites, and I used sites for buying ads on third-party websites. There aren't many ways of marketing a business that I didn't try! None of them worked.

A CHANCE MEETING WITH A GENEROUS MENTOR

Monday, 3 March, 2010, 11:25 a.m.

On March 3 at 11:25 a.m., 2010, I got my first taste of a different approach to marketing, one without promotional strategies and well outside the confines of the 4 Ps.

I had recently come across the *Sitepoint Web Design Business Kit* by Brendon Sinclair. It contained hundreds of pages with specific templates on how to build a web design agency. Given I'd spent the last five years successfully trying to do just that, this seemed like a goldmine. I read through some of the promotional pages for it, and it sounded like exactly what I needed. It was written, not by an academic or an expert trying to sell me something, but by an agency owner! It just had a different vibe to it. It didn't feel like I was being sold on some kind of old school technical marketing technique. It seemed more—organic.

Sitepoint was a big, well-known international website and authority on web development and web marketing, but as I dug more into the manual and the author, Brendon, I realized he was a local entrepreneur who actually lived and worked in the next suburb to me! I was in Burleigh Heads at the time, and he was in Palm Beach. I emailed him, and to my surprise, he not only emailed me back, but he also offered for me to come visit and grab a signed copy of the manual from him along with a coffee.

This seemed super generous to me; this was a guy who I was competing with. I was actively looking for strategies to beat him, and he's giving me advice on how to do that. Everything I thought about marketing up until that point was along the lines of "what strategies can I implement to beat people like Brendon?"

Again, I nervously headed into the coffee shop, and once again, the topic was marketing. We sat down, and on my first sip, I spilt the coffee all over myself. Brendon enjoyed that more than I did, and the coffee meeting continued. I asked him lots of questions about how to build a website agency, and he happily answered them.

I was a bit confused by his generosity, but I was also energized. When I got back to the office, I dug into the *Web Design Business Kit*, planning out all of the marketing ideas I was going to execute.

That afternoon, I was surprised by an email I received. It was from Brendon. He said, "Thanks for the catchup, it was fun, I wrote this blog post about it, and I linked back to your site." The post was funny; he was amused by me spilling coffee, and he made regular references to it. But it wasn't the content of the post or even the content of the business kit that gave me my lesson. It was the generosity of Brendon to take the time to meet with me and then write about it and link back to my website.

Back in 2010, backlinks were gold. We were beginning to understand how Google ranked websites and learning that if lots of sites linked to yours, yours would rank higher in the results. Even to this day, I know people who don't link to other people because they are so focused on their own incoming links and don't want to share the love.

In 2010, we agencies sought links from other sites, and we never deliberately linked to our competitors. The idea that this guy, who I didn't even know, would link to a competitor down the road, proactively, was something I hadn't experienced before.

Brendon was successful. His agency had been around for many years and had stayed in business and done well. He was confident enough to help anyone, even competitors. He was prepared to put everything he knew about marketing agencies into his own blog posts and into a manual for potential competitors.

He knew something that I didn't yet know. This approach of producing content, and building a brand, and being generous and not fearing competition, was in itself a marketing strategy. Certainly not the type you'd learn at university, but as it turned out, the only effective marketing strategy I've ever known.

From that day on, I fell in love with a new type of marketing.

DESIGN MATTERS

While it was my job as a web design agency owner to design websites, I had never really paid that much attention to design. That changed the following year in 2011 when Walter Isaacson released *Steve Jobs*. I struggle to read books, but I had no trouble reading this one. Released a few weeks after his death, it was a masterpiece of a book and one hell of a story.

I hadn't thought too deeply about design before reading this book, but it was Jobs' obsessive focus on design that landed for me as the biggest takeaway. Before reading the book, design seemed like something I could easily delegate to affordable contractors who knew Photoshop.

This changed upon reading the book, and while I didn't have a lot to work with at the time, I did at least have my own business and website. I decided to throw it out and start again. I relentlessly searched for great designers to help me with the site, and I found a great company overseas who had done some nice, clean-looking work.

Previously, I had either done the design work on my projects myself, or I'd hired cheap designers to hack together quick themes. This time was different. I paid way more than I was comfortable paying (a few thousand dollars at the time), and when I got the design back from the designers, I spent way more than I'd ever spent building a site, making sure I really did justice to the design.

When I launched the site, I loved it, and it looked great. For the first time, I was proud of the brand I'd built.

I don't think I sold more as a result of having a nice-looking website, but to me, this was a big turning point. I was now someone who cared deeply about how things were designed.

A GROUP WHO CARED

By 2011, I was on a new path of building my business in a new way. I found my love for design, and I was becoming a content marketing machine. I did hundreds of posts on my own blog as well as other blogs. I started looking into podcasts, ultimately launching my own. I fell in love with this concept of content marketing because it meant I no longer had to experiment with different paid strategies, and I could spend my time doing things that added value to other people. Plus, it helped my business at the same time. I fell in love with the win-win.

I also found my way into a group of like-minded entrepreneurs I came across via the hosts of a podcast called the Tropical MBA. Hosted by Dan and Ian, their group was called the Dynamite Circle, and it was an online community of small business owners like myself who were trying to build online businesses. I loved being part of the group, and the group actually turned out to be big fans of my content.

Despite all of this, my business was still struggling. In fact, it was no better than it ever was. I scraped a $40,000 wage in 2011 like every year before, and I was starting to think I couldn't make this work.

In the end, I decided I couldn't fix it, and it was around that time that Dan and Ian put on a two-week business incubator in the Philippines. I had never met them or anyone in the group in person, but there was something about listening to them each week that gave me enough confidence to fork out $2,000 (which I could barely scrape together) to attend. I packed my bags and headed to the remote island of Puerto Galera in the Philippines for a two-week stay.

On this trip, I sold my agency (for not much) and committed to building an entirely new business, a business that was more like the business of my dreams. Not one that would pay me a wage but a legit, high-growth startup.

The best idea I had was an analytics software app for small business owners, so I got to work on the idea, building out a website, a name, a signup form, and a plan to build the app. Upon my return to Australia, after finalizing the agency sale, I went back to working from home and spent the next twelve months attempting to launch this business. It was made a little bit more difficult by the fact that I'd sold my email list, social media handles, and content with my agency, so I was starting from scratch. I dove deeper into content, putting out lots of podcasts, guest posts, and posts on my own blog.

The members of the community followed along, and finally, I had a core group who cared.

WHAT'S THE STORY?

After lots of blog posts, I started to realize that one particular type of post I was writing was starting to gain traction. I started doing monthly reports and other content based on my story of going from an agency owner to starting a business of my dreams. I started garnering a small but engaged group who were following along with this content, and many of those readers were from the Dynamite Circle community. The monthly reports, specifically showing my revenue (or lack of it) for the month, were the biggest hit.

Unfortunately, before too long, it became clear that my new world-changing software startup wasn't doing too well. With my web agency, despite years of mediocre performance, I was always able to draw a wage. Now I wasn't.

Now I was losing money every month and fast running out of it. I tried a bunch of different tweaks on the idea to try to get more traction, but ultimately nothing worked. After twelve months, when I had no more money to lose, I shut it down. It was a very public failure.

I did a report every month with line charts showing my monthly recurring revenue, which at its peak got to $476, obviously not enough to sustain anything. And after twelve months, with nothing left, I kept doing the reports. It made for quite the story, and when I shut it down, I wrote a post about that, too.

This wasn't a good time for me, and I'm sure anyone who read my posts at the time could feel it in the content. Lots of small web developers and agency owners dream of following in the footsteps of Basecamp and founding a dream startup. I was out on a limb trying to do it. I'd burned the ships and had no way back. But I failed.

I had two options. My first option was to start applying for jobs, and I would need to find one in a matter of weeks. This was going to be hard since I hadn't gained many new skills in the six years since quitting, and I'd moved away from the city to where jobs in this field didn't really exist. Worse was that it would signify my ultimate failure as an entrepreneur and a six-year step backward into the corporate world if I was lucky enough to be able to get a job.

My second option wasn't great, either. I only had a few weeks of runway left, but I could somehow come up with yet another business idea and launch it if I was quick enough. I was already being ridiculed for running multiple ideas and not being able to stick to them. What's more, everyone in my small group would see this attempt to stay in the game for what it was. Desperation. I had no money either, so it wasn't like I could go all out on promotion. It was going to be a very fast and furious attempt at starting a business if I wanted to have a crack at it.

If you've read my first book, *The 7 Day Startup*, you know I went with option two: I launched a new business. It was a fixed price, unlimited jobs, WordPress support service called WP Curve. I launched it first inside the Dynamite Circle forum, and then via my blog readers and a small email list, the people who had been reading my content and following my story.

In the first week, I matched the $476 in monthly revenue that had taken me a year with my last business to accrue. By the end of the month, it was well over $1,000, which represented a nice change in my monthly income report on my blog.

From that point on, the trend continued upward. There was no more failure, only new signups, more growth, and much sexier-looking line charts on the monthly reports.

It was a comeback, under nearly impossible circumstances. Not Michael Jordan level, but in my small community of solo entrepreneurs and digital nomads, this was a pretty big deal. There were a lot of people rooting for me. I daresay there might have been a few who didn't think it would work. Either way, people were paying attention.

In that time, we pumped out hundreds of podcasts and blog posts, growing our community of followers. We also invested heavily in design, having one of the best brands and websites in the industry. And we never spent money on marketing. I gave up all forms of paid advertising and focused only on content, engaging our community, and building our brand.

It was coming together. The content was bringing us rewards for the effort, the community was more engaged than ever, and our design had us placed as a premium brand in the field of WordPress support. And as a lover of line charts, my income chart was starting to look pretty good.

By 2015, it had been on an upward trajectory for two years and was looking almost like a hockey stick growth chart, the wet dream for every startup fanboy.

By then, we had a decent size team of developers, but I hadn't ever hired anyone to help with marketing. The Dynamite Circle had this "Digital Nomad Intern" concept where people who wanted to move to Asia and live on the cheap could work for someone for a reduced rate while building their own business. It suited us well. We were ready to start delegating some of the marketing jobs but couldn't justify the cost of a full-time marketing person. We took on a group member called Kyle, a young bloke from Utah with a good heart and a lot of potential.

One of the first things he did was to look at my monthly reports. "Dan, have you noticed that your monthly income over the last ten years almost exactly matches the story arc of Cinderella?"

I certainly had not noticed that, but with a quick glance, the kid was right.

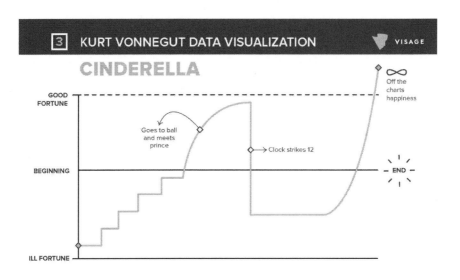

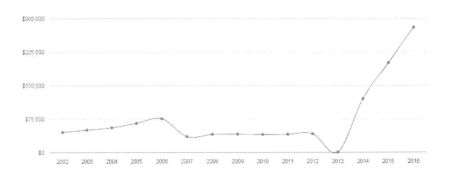

My income line chart was a story of a gradual "he's doing okay," followed by a catastrophic failure that would be seemingly impossible to come back from, then through to a drastic turnaround and accompanying exponential growth line.

It was Cinderella, suffering long-term ill fortune but with bleak hopes of improvement, presented with a major opportunity that surprisingly and disappointingly goes terribly wrong, returning her to well below the depths of misfortune, only to return bigger and better than she could imagine (and presumably forever).

It was a great lesson for me. Without even trying, I had built storytelling into my business.

My content was doing better than ever, and so was my business. Our brand was strong and respected, and in 2016, I had the biggest highlight of my career as an entrepreneur. An exit. Not just any exit, a sale to one of the world's largest internet companies, GoDaddy.

It had taken ten years, but I had finally found a way to build and market a business using techniques I never learned in textbooks.

I'd learned of the importance of content and being generous. Brendan wasn't afraid to link to me; he was more focused on creating great content for people and being generous while he did it.

I'd learned to capture the attention of a group of people and tailor that content to them. The Dynamite Circle had taught me this. Before the group, I didn't have anyone interested in my content, but as we all attempted entrepreneurship together, I had a group who were following along.

I'd learned how important design and brand was. I learned it from Jobs, and I embodied it in my first serious website. But more to the point, I felt it. It felt like something I should focus on, and it felt like the right move. Once I made the realization, I knew that design was critical to any kind of marketing success.

And the coolest part was, I'd found myself inside a great story—a story of long-term struggle and a fairytale success.

I enjoyed it at the time, but I didn't realize I'd just come across the most powerful components of marketing and business. A strategy or combination of strategies for building a business without traditional marketing and advertising. A strategy where I could ignore my university lectures and branch out on a new path. A path of generosity and fun and creativity! Marketing no longer had to be an academic, strategic exercise. Marketing was now just an offshoot of having fun at work by building a brand, telling a story, engaging a community, and creating lots of fun content.

I'd learned how to market in a very different way.

HOW MUCH SHOULD YOU SPEND ON MARKETING?

In all the years trying to figure out marketing, I had spent money on so many things that it was embarrassing. But it's normal. In fact, most companies spend a lot of money on marketing, 7.5% of all revenue on average[2].

By 2016, I'd learned that there was another way. I'd learned how to build a business without spending any money on marketing.

BUILDING ASSETS

One of the biggest lessons from my early experience as an entrepreneur was that it's not just about the marketing activity. I previously thought about marketing as something to purchase, expecting an immediate return. I guess you'd call it a transactional model. I moved to a more organic model where I focused only on putting out content, telling our story, building our brand, and engaging our community. But the results didn't come instantly; it took a very long time to get a return, much longer than you would expect from a transactional approach.

Most people treat marketing in this transactional way, i.e., "we need to do three marketing campaigns this month," or "we need to spend $50,000 on marketing this month," or "we need to spend 7.5% of our revenues on marketing."

This is like an investor saying, "I have to invest three times this month," or "I have to invest $50,000 this month," or "I have to spend

---

[2]   https://deloitte.wsj.com/cmo/2017/01/24/who-has-the-biggest-marketing-budgets/

5% of my net worth on investing this month." If an investor had this approach, they would go broke very quickly investing in bad deals.

Instead, investors look to invest only in assets that will increase their value over time. They don't expect an immediate return from the transaction. They know that building value takes time. Sure, they might get it wrong from time to time and lose money, but they have their approach, and they stick to it.

If you're investing in shares, you want a company (the asset) that will be worth more in the future than it is now. You don't expect it to go up next week as a result of today's investment.

If you're investing in private real estate, you want a house (the asset) that will be worth more in the future than it is now. You don't expect it to be worth more as soon as you sign the contract.

Money spent on Adwords gets you clicks this month, but it doesn't help you at all next month. You have to spend the money again if you want to get any benefit from this activity.

Money spent on Facebook ads or sponsored posts this month doesn't help you next month. In some cases, it might hurt. I see a lot of Facebook ads from companies who clearly can't get organic traction, and it makes me think worse of their brand. They're trying to force something on me in my social space because they aren't important enough to have my attention already.

Most marketing spend is treated like this. It's a transaction where the company puts in money and expects some kind of almost-immediate return.

But it doesn't have to be. In fact, lots of smart companies don't do this, and it gives them a pretty incredible advantage.

Your marketing time, attention, and money, if you have it, can be put into things that don't immediately die once you deploy them, assets that actually go up over time.

An investor's approach to marketing.

COMPOUNDING ASSETS

Investors look for assets that will go up over time, and their best investments will do it consistently year on year. That's called compounding.

The concept of compounding is simple. Growth on its own is great, but growth on growth is even better. In a simple example, if you invested $10,000 at a 12% annual growth rate, you would have $11,200 at the end of the year. You can then take those profits and spend them on beer. That's cool.

If you keep repeating this pattern, you'll end up with $22,000 after 10 years ($12,000 profit). That's a lot of beer!

But if you don't take the money and spend it on beer and the interest accrues on the whole amount (i.e., in year 1 you get 12% on $11,200 instead of $10,000), you end up with $31,058 in that time[3]. That's $21,058 in profit, almost double the amount to spend on beer if you are patient enough to wait.

Compounding growth is well understood by entrepreneurs. It's chased after like the holy grail and for good reason.

With WP Curve, we had a benchmark of growing monthly recurring revenue by a mere 10% per month. The first month the revenue was $476, so all we had to do was grow it to $524, which was one new customer in that month. If we hit this target, we would be a $1m business in just over 2.5 years.

And that's exactly what happened. We grew by 10% each month for two years and turned a rushed idea into a million-dollar company. That's the power of compounding.

COMPOUND MARKETING

Our current understanding of marketing doesn't really capture the power of what's possible when you focus your marketing efforts on asset-building activities that compound over time. We divide marketing into disciplines. You do SEO, or you do Google Ads, or

---

[3]   https://www.investors.asn.au/education/investment-basics/power-of-compounding/

you do content marketing. Maybe we do all of these things, but they are still all separate things.

Content marketing is great, but it doesn't completely cover what is possible with compounding asset-building marketing strategies. You can make a lot of great content and still have people who don't feel right about your brand.

Branding is great and super important, but it doesn't capture the whole mindset because most of the power of a brand is subconscious. What about all the actions that have to happen in the real world to generate that brand love?

We need a new definition of the types of marketing activities that are designed to build assets that compound against each other and over time.

By way of a simple definition:

Compound marketing is putting marketing effort into things that go up in value.

The coolest part is that it doesn't have to be one thing. We can undertake multiple compounding investments at the same time. We don't have to wait a year for the compounding to take place.

THE 4 COMPOUND MARKETING STRATEGIES

It was a long and sometimes painful process for me to learn that there were marketing strategies that didn't involve short-term transactions, and they could be the most powerful ones of all. They were strategies that would build value over time and compound year on year.

But over those lessons, I learned the power of brand, the necessity of story, the criticality of content, and the purpose of community. These were the four strategies: me spending time obsessing over the design philosophy of Steve Jobs, finding myself in the middle of a story, finding a group of entrepreneurs who cared, and my relentless publishing of content. This was what compounded. This was the strategy.

1. Brand

2. Storytelling

3. Content

4. Community

Or, if you think about it sequentially: build a brand and tell a story via content to your community.

1

BRAND

At the risk of turning this thing into a textbook, let's spend some time figuring out what brand is. When you look into common definitions of branding, you come across ones like this:

> *"A name, term, design, symbol, or any other feature that identifies one seller's good or service as distinct from those of other sellers."*[4] American Marketing Association

And they're not wrong. When you think of a brand, you probably think of a logo or a product from that company. Forbes keeps a list of the world's most valuable brands, and they have a crack at valuing them[5].

#1 is Apple. When I think of Apple, I think of that super-simple little Apple logo, I think about my phone, and I think about how grateful I am for the keyboard on my MacBook Pro that cops this level of constant abuse required to write a book (early 2015 model, thank god).

#2 is Google. I think of that hideous logo.

---

[4] https://www.ama.org/the-definition-of-marketing-what-is-marketing/

[5] https://www.forbes.com/powerful-brands/list/

#3 is Microsoft. I think of their enterprise-like logo.

#4 is Amazon. I think about that little arrow logo, my Alexa, and my Kindle.

#5 is Facebook. I think blue and think about the Facebook and Instagram apps.

$6 is Coca Cola. I think of that retro swirly lettering.

#7 is Disney. I think about the old-school Walt Disney logo, the theme parks, and their new streaming service, Disney Plus.

The name or the logo makes me immediately think of these things.

But this doesn't really capture the brand, does it. Brand is not so much about what you think; it's more about how you feel.

When I think of Apple, I feel good; I feel calm. I think of nice clean, simple lines and beautifully designed products. I think of how fast my new phone is and how good the photo I just took was. I think about the six books and hundreds of blog posts I've written on MacBooks. A hell of a lot of sacrifice and torment went into making me feel like that. It feels like every product they release is heavily criticized, but when I think of Apple, I feel good, and I think perhaps Steve Jobs knew that this was the most important thing.

Amazon feels like a super useful friend. I listen to music on Alexa; I read books on my Kindle; I started listening to a book this morning on Audible (an Amazon service). Every time I want something, Amazon is there. It just seems like an essential service that's part of my life, and it helps get me things I need way easier than before. They even host my website. I feel good about Amazon.

Disney makes me think of my kids; I'm happy immediately when I hear that word and see the logo. I remember my childhood. I think back to all the times in the movies and on the couch with my kids watching Marvel, Disney, and Pixar movies. I think back to visiting Disneyland in Hong Kong, one of the most fun days I've had. I feel good when I think of Disney.

When I think of Facebook, I feel a bit dirty. I originally wrote this section on 2 June 2020:

Facebook employees are staging a first-of-its-kind virtual walk-out protesting Mark Zuckerberg's lack of action around censoring violence-promoting and non-factual information posted on the platform. The company has been more successful than ever, but it's had a hard run with election interference, hacking scandals, and mental health problems, to name a few. They've copied or bought every competitor, and their CEO isn't exactly the most relatable character. I use Facebook and their apps a lot. They are useful, but I don't feel good about it. To me, that is Facebook's brand right now. Facebook has a branding problem, and it has nothing to do with a logo or a product. It has to do with how people feel about it.

I'm not one for making long-term predictions, but the better part of me likes to believe that the brands that people love are the ones that thrive in the long run.

How people feel about your business or your products is the essence of your brand. Your logo and your products and your name spoken in conversation will induce those feelings, but what those feelings induce depends on how much work you do to cultivate a healthy brand.

Your brand is the cornerstone of every decision you make in your business from the day you make it. It's your DNA, and everything you put out from that point forward reflects what your brand truly is.

Yes, it's your name, and your logo, and your products, but it's also your story, and it's every blog post you write, every design you release, every employee you hire, every employee you fire, everything you say "yes" to, and everything you say "no" to.

Your brand is who you are as a company. So, yeah—it's important.

WHY YOU CAN'T DELEGATE BRANDING

I'm always wary of a field where there is literally no barrier to entry, and anyone can call themselves an expert. But it seems very common for entrepreneurs to choose designers fairly randomly like it wasn't a big decision.

On the list of skills that entrepreneurs should never delegate, branding would be top of the list. People treat branding like it's a job to delegate to the designer that your Facebook friend recommended. Do you really want to delegate your identity to a local design contractor?

Do you want to run a $20 competition to determine who gets to decide how someone feels about your entire company?

If you are a smart entrepreneur, you don't want this. Branding is something you should own yourself. And I don't mean you should fire up Photoshop and crank out your company logo. I mean, you should understand branding so well and respect your brand so much that no one will make decisions about it other than you.

Of course, get advice and help from legit experts who can make beautiful designs and create and build great brands. But only get that advice and service once you yourself have a good handle on what branding is, and you know great design from poor design. Trust me, asking your friends what they like is not the way to do this.

THE WAY COMPANIES THINK ABOUT BRANDING IS CHANGING

I read a book on the topic of story and branding just this week, and right at the start, one of the most highlighted passages of the book stated, "The fact is, pretty websites don't sell things. Words sell things.[6]" How things have changed in just a few short years!

This way of thinking used to be the standard among marketers. Marketers wrote design off as a fun thing that crazy creative people did with the only possible outcome being things being a bit prettier. It was never regarded as a serious sales tool. I've never met a copywriter who advised on heavily investing in design. On the contrary, most pushed for as little design as possible on the basis that this method "converted better." Design was looked at as a bit of an enemy for people trying to sell things. What was valued most was getting the quickest sale and selling to the most amount of people at that time. Or, as Seth Godin recently put it, *"Most people in online marketing are selfish short-term, lying, narcissistic profit-maximizing, and don't*

---

[6] https://www.amazon.com.au/Building-Story-Brand-Clarify-Customers/dp/0718033329

care about building trust or giving people dignity and are looking for the latest scam."[7]

Building great brands and great companies generally takes a long time, and design is a long-term play.

These days, design has become a major differentiator for big brands and arguably a bare necessity for serious startups. Design is regarded as a skill so important that equity in potentially unicorn-level startup companies is given away in return for design skills.

Entrepreneurs trying to build real value aren't as concerned about immediate sales; they are concerned about building a valuable brand over time. Have a look at the Tesla website with the huge amazing images with two to three-word headings and no more text. I want to buy a Tesla more than I want to buy anything else, and it has nothing to do with the words on their website. I love their brand.

BRANDS ARE STORIES

We've spent a long time talking about the importance of building a story for your company, your customers, or your products. Your brand is central to that story.

When people visualize your founding story, you want them to see your brand and product at the end. When people think about your customer stories, you want them to visualize your customers holding your branded product and using your products. When people think about your product, you want them to recognize the logo, but more importantly, you want them to feel what your brand is about.

The stories you feel reinforce the brand, and the brand backs up the story. We have a beer at Black Hops called G.O.A.T (Greatest Of All Time). I'll give you the story of the beer later, but suffice to say that with that name, the beer has to look good! When I think of G.O.A.T., I think of the first product photo we did, which included four normal beers in a semi-circle and a beautiful orange hazy G.O.A.T. with a spotlight shining on it showing that it was best in class. When we introduced the beer into the core range, we

---

[7]   https://productiveinsights.com/seth-godin-on-marketing/

did so in our first all-black can, simple and sleek with sharp silver slivers of our logo and the words G.O.A.T. shining through from the substrate of the can. The beer brewed with high expectations had to look the part.

Continuing the product story through to the design of the product is exactly what Compound Marketing is. The story alone is powerful, and the brand alone is sexy, but combined, the brand reminds the customer of the story every time the product is consumed. That's what I call a good investment!

HOW TO ACHIEVE GREAT DESIGN ON A BUDGET

At some point, you will have to get some external help with building your brand, and expert branding doesn't come cheap. Every single year of my fourteen years as an entrepreneur, I've struggled with the decision of which designer to choose and how much to spend. I've never had the luxury of finding the world's best and being able to afford to get them to work on my brand. I've had to be scrappy and set my expectations high but try my best to achieve great design with a fraction of the money spent.

A lot of entrepreneurs are faced with the same decision, and I worry they just choose a cheap option and accept the result. I want to discourage you from taking this path and instead take this on as your own challenge to achieve great design without the outlay.

PUT IN THE WORK

In 2002, a year after graduating in human resources, I was working in an HR consultancy in a graduate role. I was very grateful to have a graduate job in my field of study, but I wasn't particularly excited about the work. Through an onsite placement, I met the son of a lady I worked with who was studying design at college. I was 22, he was even younger, and he'd started at college straight out of school. We got to talking about design.

I loved these conversations, and at one point, I asked, "How do you feel about teaching me how to do design?" I said I'd be happy to pay him $20 per lesson. It sounds a little stingy now, but at the time, for a young guy, it wasn't a bad way to spend an hour or two.

He came to my house and started to show me how to use Photoshop 6, an image editing tool that was fast becoming the standard for designing brands and websites. I had a shitty old computer and Photoshop ran like a dog, but I loved these nights. I learned how to use the various tools and tried to get my head around how someone could possibly make a design out of nothing. I'd never been someone who drew or did anything design related, so it was all new to me.

These initial lessons led me to take up an online course in multimedia and embark on my own personal efforts to learn about design. Through the course, and mainly through teaching myself, I learned Photoshop, Fireworks (which I very much preferred), and eventually, other tools like Illustrator, InDesign, Flash, Dreamweaver, and more.

I had changed employers, but by then, my job was still in human resources, albeit in a different section of online learning. I'd managed to morph my role in the government from one working on boring HR projects to one building online learning courses using my self-taught skills in design and multimedia.

2006 was the year I quit Queensland Rail to start a business designing and building websites. I threw myself in the deep end. My first project was to design a website for a flashy HR consultancy, and yep, you guessed it, it was the one I previously worked at. I took all the photos myself, designed the structure of the site myself, designed every page, and coded the pages in HTML and JavaScript. I'm not sure I've since felt quite as satisfied as when I built that drop-down menu that behaved in Netscape and Internet Explorer!

More jobs came, and before I knew it, I'd gone from an HR consultant to a full-time web designer/developer.

I was never particularly good at design, but I've never stopped loving design. When I stopped designing things myself, I didn't delegate it entirely. I now knew a hell of a lot about it, so I knew my shortcomings, I knew good design from bad, and I appreciated great design. In my current position, I try to delegate design. The people I delegate to get pissed off that I won't let it go.

Over the years, those skills have helped more than I would have ever expected.

I don't think every entrepreneur needs to learn Photoshop, but I can tell you it doesn't hurt. Those skills continue to be useful to this day in a practical sense, but more importantly, they have given me a foundation to understand at least the practical elements of design.

CARE ABOUT DESIGN

In my experience, entrepreneurs don't care about design. They don't value it.

How does something become something when it was previously nothing? This is a mystery that is worthy of a lifelong pursuit. It confuses a lot of entrepreneurs and ends up in the "too hard basket." But it shouldn't.

You should understand it, appreciate it, and respect it. When it is done well, you should be able to see it. And you should never delegate it without supreme confidence that the person who's looking after it can see it. You certainly should never "permission-seek" it from other people.

I will delegate almost everything else, but it's a big call to delegate your brand.

Your work might be very different from my work. It might be studying architecture, it might be falling in love with a certain style of art, it might be making food, or it might be following artists on Instagram or Dribbble. Whatever it is, educate yourself on design. It's a good investment.

When I talk about this, I'm not saying don't ever hire a designer. I hire many designers regularly, and I work with astonishingly talented people who can produce things that I could never dream of producing. But the designer doesn't ultimately have ownership of what gets produced. The job of the entrepreneur is to accept that the designer will get all the credit, but be the owner. Sometimes, this is an uncomfortable position.

There have been many times where I've had to invest an uncomfortable amount of money on design. Every time it worked, I saw it as my personal success, and every time it failed, I saw it as my personal failure. Other people will see it differently, but the mentality of the brand-conscious entrepreneur is "you own the brand," regardless. It's on you. Allow the designers to get credit when it's great, and when it's not great, it's your fault. That's the curse of being an entrepreneur in many ways outside of design, and it's no different here. It is 100% on you.

I've never regretted caring about design, and the amount of entrepreneurs I meet who seem not to care about design tells me that this is a big differentiator.

Consider: You will be miles ahead of the average entrepreneur if you know about design, care about design, and don't settle until you are happy with the design.

THE 3 COMMANDMENTS OF GOOD DESIGN

As you will read throughout this section, design can get very complicated and painful. When designing anything, I encourage you to stick by these three commandments regardless of how hard or how easy they are to achieve.

1. It has to look good to your buyers. This is the point of design; it's supposed to look good, which is often harder than it sounds.

2. It feels right. Something that looks good doesn't necessarily feel right for the project at hand. Design has to feel right.

3. It works. Design is a practical discipline. You won't enjoy living with a design that looks good, feels right, but doesn't work in practice.

THE DESIGN PROBLEM SCALE

Here's a pertinent question: How hard will it be to solve your design issue? Some problems are harder to solve than others; there's a scale.

Once you have a decent understanding of design, you should have a good handle on where your particular design problem sits on the scale. And this matters.

Some brands lend themselves well to executing a nice simple design, and some don't. And since you are the entrepreneur, it's your choice! If you choose a simple brand name or product name that will lend itself to a nice design, it might make your life a lot easier. If you choose a brand that is hard to design for, it might be a tough road ahead. That's not to say it won't be a worthy trip, but you should know what you're in for before you take it.

I've launched lots of brands with varying degrees of success—and even more varying degrees of failure. And within those brands, I've launched many products. Sometimes, the design falls together nicely. Those are good times. Sometimes it's impossible to resolve with the budget we have and the designer we have and the constraints we have, and the brand we have. Other times it's almost impossible, but worth a hard slog.

I like to think that, over the years, I've become better at spotting this before it happens.

These days, when I start thinking about a name for a business, a brand, or a product, I immediately think about how it might look. I try not to think of obvious designs but more try to think of things a designer might think of. Are there some neat metaphors? Is there a nice easy non-cliche solution to this design problem? Can we make something that looks simple and elegant with these words, or is that going to be very difficult? Is this either going to be a really obvious cliché or a design that is near impossible to elegantly resolve? These are big decisions and often happen very early, so it pays to have the capacity to understand design early on.

Once you understand and appreciate design, you'll think this way, and it will save you a hell of a lot of trouble!

When we decided on the name "Black Hops," the decision was based purely on the name being cool. But the design process to get from there through to the greatest, sexiest-looking can of all time was a long and painful one.

First, I had a crack myself, going down the most obvious cliché path, finding a military font in Google and writing out the words "Black Hops" and pressing send. It was fun, but it didn't have the hallmarks of a great beer brand. It was tough because people loved our brand and our logo and convincing my business partners to spend money on a whole new brand wasn't easy.

Since the business had no money, I decided to pay for a rebrand myself, handing out $4,000 to a respected local agency to come up with a new brand for us. I was confident that design was worth the investment, and despite not having the money, this was something we needed. The agency did a shit job, and after months of back and forth, we ended the project in a very unsatisfactory way. Bridges were burnt, the brand was in no better shape, and I was $4,000 poorer. I'd also failed in my main job to help us build a great brand for Black Hops, which I was supposedly the expert in.

The problem was that this was a particularly hard branding problem to solve. It was very high on the design problem scale—a big problem!

The obvious angle was a brute force military style logo, but this wasn't what the average beer drinker wanted when they walked into the bottle shop. And while we were constantly being told people love our brand, I at least had the foresight to see that this brand was not going to be enough to get us to where we really wanted to be: a mainstream choice for craft beer customers at the bottle shop.

I wanted something more elegant and refined, but something that still told our story and preserved some military elements.

After a few more months, once the business raised some money, I convinced the other founders to try again at a redesign. Despite embarrassing myself on the last effort, they agreed, and I started looking for some help. This time, after an RSI-inducing scroll session on Dribbble, I found a talented designer who looked like he could help. He'd done beer work before, and his style was elegant and recognizable. On top of that, he lived locally! We met up with him, did a tour of a local bottleshop, and started the project of redesigning Black Hops.

After weeks of back and forth, some hits and some misses, we arrived at an awesome-looking brand for Black Hops. A unique, hand-drawn Black Hops scripted logo with a military-inspired chevron and a unique font for the word "BREWERY."

The logo was the start, and that sometimes painful, continual struggle to come up with great design for the brand, for the products, for merch, for new releases, etc. continues to this day. We recently ordered beanies and flannelette shirts after about five years in the making. It's not an easy brand to make work!

Black Hops wasn't easy at the start, and it's not easy for every product we put out. But it's a unique brand, and the struggle pays off. Our product doesn't look like everyone else's, and we hope it doesn't feel like everyone else's.

But that's somewhat easy to say in our sixth year of business. Having that kind of brand for a new company is a lot of pain.

Some design problems aren't this complicated. Sometimes you can come up with a simple name that is a really nice fit for a simple and obvious design. This can be great, too; it doesn't necessarily have to be a struggle. For some things, you don't want to struggle.

When we put a small batch beer out, I often think about how it will look before we decide on the name. There might only be fifty cartons made, but we'll have a brand name for the beer, a well-written description, a fully branded can and decal, a custom recipe, and maybe a professional photoshoot. We do these beers weekly, so we can't go through months-long design processes to come up with something decent. Sometimes, it makes a lot of sense to choose something that is very easily executed, and I can just tell the designer, "Do this."

Putting yourself in a situation where you have a simple design problem is a great thing. If you arrive at a design that looks great, feels right, and works, then there's no need to feel guilty and feel like you need to dig into it further. Take it as a win.

DON'T GET FEEDBACK

Bad feedback is the enemy of good design. If you've heard anything I've written so far about design, you'll understand that, if you aren't a designer turned entrepreneur, understanding design is a lot of work. How many entrepreneurs do you think put in this work?

Not many.

How many people who aren't entrepreneurs put in this work?

Even less.

Solving design problems requires a lot of effort, sometimes a long and painful process and a huge amount of understanding of the design problem.

It makes me sick how much the average entrepreneur de-values design. You can't just ask your friends which logo they prefer and think that solves a design problem.

Why would you want to get feedback on design from people who don't understand design? Doing this just shows that you don't care about design. If you care about it, you wouldn't post three logos on Facebook and ask people to vote on the best one.

Feedback is a cop-out. It's a sign that you don't want to take responsibility for this crucially important job. It's like when new entrepreneurs ask their friends if they think their business idea is a good idea. It's a complete waste of time.

Put up a page and ask people to pay; you will soon find out whether or not it's a good idea.

I love it when people say you should ask your customers because they're the only people that really matter. WTF? Are you crazy? You think customers are going to magically become supreme designers and gift you with all the amazing and free design advice? Please. Unless your business is called Adobe or Sketch or InVision, your customers aren't designers. DO NOT ASK THEM!

Ken Kocienda was a software engineer and designer at Apple for fifteen years. He said, "Google couldn't decide between two blues, so they're testing forty-one shades between each blue to see which one performs better. At Apple, we never would have dreamed of doing that, and we never staged any A/B tests for any of the software on the iPhone." To the question of "Why does a product work like it does?" Apple's answer was, "This is how we think it works best. We like it this way. We developed a point of view, and we were willing to ship our opinions."[8]

Finding a design resolution is your job. It's your job to find the right designer to work with and the right process to follow, and it's up to you to back yourself to find the right result. It's your job not to delegate it until you are 100% comfortable. It's your job to choose the right level of difficulty of design problems in the right circumstances.

It's your job to own up to the fact that it won't always work. And when it doesn't work, it will be your fault. When it does work, well, that's when the designer gets all the credit. And those talented people deserve it.

HAVE A GOOD DESIGN PROCESS

One of the big reasons design projects fail is because entrepreneurs don't understand the process, or they don't care about the process. Design is not a matter of randomly making something pretty to look at. The best designers don't even start thinking about what something will look like until they've been through a long and often challenging process.

Sometimes arriving at a design is very painful. There's a lot of back and forth and a lot of unhappy people, and even when you launch, you aren't sure. Months later, once the pain subsides, it grows on you, and you realize that you and the designer were so deep in the problem that you didn't realize the beauty of what you created. That's when you have yourself a good design. If you are designing products, often you don't get this moment until you see the product out in the wild, free from any biases, and you can see how people interact with it, what they say as they talk about it to their friends and show them.

---

[8]   https://twitter.com/kocienda/status/1289204980281307136?fbclid=IwAR2qkJ
f4KGzYq1uXWmwOGhlGtBeAL6lHovkzU6-50AuBnJBwlLYnuxynUGk

Design problems don't always have to be this painful. Sometimes, they are easy, but in every case, the process is important.

Some design problems are ripe for cheesy and literal design solutions. A book or a short-run product might be a good target for a cheap design solution. Design comp sites and cheap designers could be good choices for these sorts of projects. I don't think you necessarily need to spend tens of thousands of dollars on every design project.

The 7 Day Startup (my first book) might have a logo of the number 7 or a rocketship to signify launch (very literal and very overused). That would probably work fine as a small project or a book cover. I went with a slingshot, but you get the point.

Black Hops might have a Black Hop and the letters BH written in military font. For our first beer release, that would probably be fine, but for a brand that has to live on in the hearts and minds of thousands of customers over years and years, it won't cut it.

I studied architecture for a year full-time at university in my 30s, and it was a real eye-opener. I'm a practical person who thought it would be fun to design houses, so I thought architecture might be for me. But the whole of the first year was so abstract and strange that I dropped out. Every design was a metaphor, every solution was a story, but I just wanted to design a fucking veranda!

But this is the stuff that great designers obsess over. It's a real, legitimate skill. Like a great writer or a book or a movie, they tell you one story, but the thing that grips you is something underlying so deep you can't even see it.

This magic can come about by following a great design process.

I can't quantify what a good design process is. The best I can do is lay out a few key requirements.

You need to deeply understand design, and the designer has to deeply understand your business. Peter Thiel, the billionaire entrepreneur and investor, founder of PayPal and Palintir, and an early investor and current board member of Facebook, said, "Every great entrepreneur is first and foremost a designer."[9] I think I've made

---

[9]   https://www.amazon.com.au/Zero-One-Notes-Startups-Future/dp/0804139296

the point that this is something you need to invest in and requires a lot of ongoing work. It's something worth caring about.

The designer has to have the courage to push her ideas on you, and you have to have the courage to push your own ideas back on her. She might be really excited about something, but it doesn't mean you have to be, and visa versa. This process can be painful, but with the right designer who's open to feedback from someone they respect from a design point of view, it can yield a great result.

You normally can't just go for an easy literal interpretation of the problem. If you want the design to last and be more meaningful, you need to dig into metaphors and abstractions. Let the design sit with you for a while before you decide if you love it. If you love it straight away, it might not be a great sign.

Look for a story or mood in the design. Consider how the design makes you feel, not just how it looks. This is the stuff that really matters. This is especially true if you are designing products. You might have a really sexy design, but it just doesn't feel the way it should for your product.

Dive deep. If your designer requires you to go for a walk in the park or take you onsite or go to the Amazon to do an ayahuasca ceremony, then do it. These are signs the designer has a good handle on the process. (The ayahuasca comment was a joke, but you get my point).

Find a designer you trust and pay attention to the process. Getting from idea to well-executed design is not easy and requires a lot of thought.

Literal logo interpretations and cheap design competitions rarely result in effective brand representation. Only a solid process will get you that result.

Another thing I've noticed working with designers for many years is that sometimes a bit of time doesn't hurt. Let the designer present the idea and justify their decisions and don't give feedback on the spot. Sit on it for a day or two, consider their points, look at it from different angles, and then get back to them. I've done this a few times, and the designers have gone off and designed totally different versions because they think they haven't nailed it, so better you explain up front that this is your process. A bit of time can provide a lot of clarity when it comes to design.

DON'T GET TOO CARRIED AWAY

In 2016, Uber undertook a radical rebranding. Having grown up fast from a few luxury cars in San Francisco to a platform spanning 400 cities in 65 countries, they decided their well recognized U logo no longer cut it. It was too literal. They couldn't just say UBER and have a U logo anymore. They needed to dive deeper. Plus, they had the money to do it after multiple funding rounds, including a $7.3 billion-dollar round the year before from Saudi Arabia's Public Investment Fund.[10]

Design-wise, they needed something more sophisticated. More grown up. Something with meaning.

The refresh was a long time coming. Their designer at the time, Shalin Amin, had his eyes on a redesign since 2012 and finally gained the support of the CEO, Travis Kalanic, toward the end of 2013 to start discussions with agencies about a full rebrand. Amin and Kalanic spent eighteen months coming up with brand pillars and by mid-2015 had a strong internal design team and had moved away from the idea of working with brand agencies.

After hiring one of Google's designers, they workshopped 200 different fonts to replace the Uber text. They sketched hundreds of icons, and when progress wasn't looking good, their head designer organized a week-long retreat and challenged the designers to develop a concept, not just an icon. Something more meaningful. Something with a story. The team began to focus on a blog post that Uber founder Travis Kalanick had written where he compared Uber's culture to a combination of bits and atoms.[11] Bits represented the machine efficiency involved in Uber's mapping and dispatch software. The atoms represented people.

---

[10]   https://craft.co/uber/funding-rounds

[11]   https://www.uber.com/newsroom/bits-atoms-2

After many more months, trips around the world, and much collaboration within the design team, Uber unveiled its new identity that consisted, more or less, of a dot in the middle of a circle.[12]

The new branding was called bizarre by Fortune Magazine and was widely criticized.[13] It was savagely over-cooked, over-thought, embedded with so much underlying meaning that it confused people. The U that everyone knew was now a dot. Who benefited from that?

Two years later, Uber went back to an agency, Wolff Olins, a renowned brand consultancy founded in 1965 in London, and replaced the brand again. This time, the famous Uber app changed to four letters, U, B, E, and R.

In short, they spent eight years, and god knows how much money, trying to build meaning into their logo and ended up with their business name in letters.

Design can so easily be overthought, particularly if you listen too much to designers. I don't care how much something means; what means the most is that it looks good, it feels right, and it works.

For small businesses, this is especially true. Most small businesses have horrible design because (a) the founder knows nothing about design and doesn't know any better, or (b) their designer is given full control and comes up with something average.

You have a great opportunity to produce something with a bit of effort that looks great and puts you ahead of 99% of other businesses. If you achieve that, it's a big enough win. Don't get too carried away to a point where you forget the basics of what's really important.

LOOK AT WHAT THE EXPERTS DO

After reading about how a $60b company can waste eight years on a crap design, this might seem to be a hard pill to swallow, but believe it or not, there is a lot you can learn from big brands and design experts.

---

[12] https://www.wired.com/2016/02/the-inside-story-behind-ubers-colorful-redesign/
[13] https://fortune.com/2016/02/02/new-uber-logo/

Back when I was first learning about design, I found another mentor in Rob, who was a website contractor at the government agency I was working for. He was working for someone else in the department, and I noticed on his laptop that he was working on a website. My eye was drawn to the nice round tabs he'd designed. I was so perplexed about how you could even get to the decision to design something like that. Where do you start to end up with nice rounded tabs as your navigation? I was interested in both how you made something that looked that cool but also why you would choose a tab over another navigation element. And yes, I realize how much of a loser I must have been to care about this sort of shit at twenty-five.

I asked him embarrassingly, "How did you make those tabs?" He said, "I went online and loaded five other websites from big company startups at the time and looked at what they did." From memory, it was Microsoft at the time who was using that tab design, and he liked it, screenshotted it, and used Photoshop to figure out exactly how they did it. He didn't use the exact design, but he figured out how they did it to help him come up with his own tabs for his own project. Feels a bit like stealing, but as Austin Kleon said in his book *Steal Like an Artist*: "Every new idea is just a mashup or a remix of one or more previous ideas." I'm not advocating stealing other designs. I do think that looking at what's out there and using it as a starting point of a very normal and solid way to approach design.[14]

Microsoft probably spent millions of dollars coming up with that design, and he could do some small version of it in a few minutes that looked a lot better than most websites. As he worked through the rest of the project, I'm sure he came back to it and tweaked it, it evolved, and by the end, it looked nothing like their website.

I like to look at startup websites like Crunchbase and AngelList. If you just find a list of the startups who are hiring or raising lots of money or exploding in growth, you will find a valuable trail of design work by the best and brightest designers. These are the companies where people want to work and where the best designers are going.

---

[14]   https://www.amazon.com.au/Steal-Like-Artist-Things-Creative/dp/0761169253

Consider this. If most founders are happy to go on Facebook and ask their friends for the best out of three designs, wouldn't it make way more sense to at least look at what some of the most valuable companies in the world are doing? Or some of the world's most innovative startups who are hiring the world's best and brightest designers? Not to say that their executions are always right or right for your business or your product, but you can bet you will learn more from these places than you would from a crappy designer or your Facebook friends.

USE YOUR GREATEST ASSETS

One of the most frustrating things for me when I used to build websites was clients giving me awful images. I tried my best to build great websites, but they ended up looking shit because the client's photos were shit.

A mate of mine at the time, and another one of my early mentors in design, Liam worked for EA. He looked after their websites and online activities and everything he designed was phenomenal. Huge, larger-than-life characters of Muhammad Ali and Mike Tyson surrounded beautiful large text and shiny gel-like buttons promoting their latest boxing game. These websites were so good that I had to know how the hell he made them.

At the time, I had switched from Photoshop to Fireworks for web design because I found it so much more intuitive. You could just see something, mouse over it (and you could tell), and you could click things, and it would select them. Revolutionary, I know, but still a feature that Photoshop doesn't have. But I digress.

I assumed my mate Liam was a Photoshop genius to come up with these phenomenal websites.

I hounded him for info regularly (sorry, Liam, if you read this so many years later), and one day, he showed me the source files for the design of these websites. It turned out that he used Fireworks, and the websites were, for the most part, gigantic epic images provided by EA, some nice text, and a few buttons. Not to discount my friend's skills as a designer, he was awesome, but it really did show me the importance of great assets in design.

In my world as a brewery owner, our biggest asset is our product, the beer. We put a huge amount of effort into the names of the beers, the type of beer, the story, the quality of the liquid, and, of course, the design of the label. Once we are happy with all of that, we pay an agency a reasonable amount of money to get a really sick photo of the beer.

We release a lot of beers, over 100 this year, but not every beer will get this treatment. But I can tell you that when we put all of that effort into the product, the label, and the photo, the result is immensely better than if we don't. The content we put out (mostly social media these days as opposed to website content) does infinitely better, and the beer sells infinitely faster.

Some of the sexiest websites and branding resources are made by the companies that make the sexiest products. Have a look at the Tesla website. Other than buttons and menu items, there are only two words on the entire screen when it loads (at the time of writing), "Model 3." The rest is stupidly sexy photos of their beautiful cars and solar products. They don't need a great web designer; they need a photographer and a developer.

Get some nice assets, and you are well on your way to having nice design.

PRIORITIZE VISUALS

Ever have a favorite song where you know every word and sing along every time, and then one day, someone tells you the bizarre story behind it, and you realize you know nothing about what this song means? Either the artist is so clever that they sent you subconscious messages of meaning through obscure lyrics, or you just liked the way it sounded and really didn't give a shit what it was about.

I think it's mostly the latter. Sure, there are some examples of amazing songs with amazing meanings and backstories that also present as super catchy tunes; they come along a few times a decade. But between those rare unicorn songs, there are loads of great songs that just sound bloody good. How many people try to create a unicorn song like this and end up with some butchered shitty mess of a song full of meaning that isn't fun to listen to? Probably 99.99% of all songs written.

I think design is the same. Occasionally, you'll see a brand or a product where they absolutely nail a flawless design with underlying meanings and metaphors that also stands out as a sexy as fuck product, but it's super rare. Most times, trying to create something like this fails, even often for the world's best designers.

Steve Jobs famously paid renowned designer Paul Rand $100,000 to design a logo for NeXT Computer, the business he started after being booted out of Apple.[15] Paul put together a one-hundred-page document outlining the process and final design. Have you seen the logo? I don't care how much meaning was embedded into that thing; it's hideous.[16]

One thing I know for sure is that people like nice looking things. See the first commandment of design: It has to look good.

It goes for every aspect of life. People like nice-looking people, they like nice-looking cars, they like nice-looking buildings, and they like nice-looking clothes. And, of course, they like nice-looking brands and websites and social media accounts and products and marketing collateral.

In case the Uber story wasn't enough of a cautionary tale about what happens when you try to make something too meaningful, just use this basic test. Does it look good? Design should look good, and if you've put in the work as an entrepreneur to know the difference, then you will know if it does or if it doesn't.

REMEMBER DESIGN IS CONTEXTUAL

We can't get too carried away with our sexy designs without considering how and where and why and who the design is presented to. Designers are really good at making things look sexy in a concept proof. Have

---

[15]   https://en.wikipedia.org/wiki/NeXT_Computer

[16]   https://www.logodesignlove.com/next-logo-paul-rand

a look at the designers' community site, Dribbble; there's never a single bad looking concept.[17]

I can't say I get one-hundred-page concepts from the designers I work with as Steve Jobs did, but I do often get really sexy, well-presented mockups. Quite often in my world of beer, I'll get 3D mockups of cans with beautiful background textures and drop shadows, and you'll instantly fall in love with the design.

But context is everything. I always have to remember that the designs we do are never seen on the screen and never seen in a document. They rarely have nice neat drop shadows and supporting backing images. Our core range beers sit in a fridge with a bright light at the top loaded with thousands of other cans.

Our limited releases are more often seen on social media. They aren't sent to bottle shops, and they sell out so fast they are barely seen at the brewery, and by the time people come in to buy them, it wouldn't matter. We post the beer with a nice-looking image of, hopefully, a sexy looking can, a cool story, and a great beer idea, and all of that is what sells the beer. The design of these labels needs to work well in a stand-alone social media post.

All of our beers end up in fridges or eskies and are held in hands and consumed from above while staring at the top of the boring silver lid. All of this is context that has to be understood by the designer and the business owner.

The "lack of context" mistake gets made all the time. People don't think about where and when their design will be needed. People design logos with dark backgrounds and then realize that almost every place you put a logo is white and having a dark background surrounding a logo is causing you a major branding issue every time you use your brand.

People put together brands for print purposes and approve them online, not even taking the time to print even a rough version to see how it looks in the real world. Every time I get a beer label, I print it and sticky tape it to a can. It's the only way to really understand how it looks, how it feels, and if it works.

---

[17]   https://dribbble.com/

Context matters, so make sure you are thinking about where your design will be seen before you get too excited about how sexy it looks.

LET DESIGNERS JUSTIFY THEIR WORK

If it sounds like I'm being harsh on designers in all of this, I'm really not. I love the designers I work with, and there's very little in my job that gets me more excited than when I see a new sexy-as-fuck design for a new beer release. And if it wasn't beer, it would be something else. I'd happily work with designers on designing anything as my main job forever and be very content.

So I want to give designers the benefit of the doubt here and say that they should be given a proper opportunity to present their work. Once you have a great relationship with your designer, they might be able to crank out designs, email you, get the tick, and send it to the printer. But at first, it's probably not going to be that simple.

If your designer wants to meet with you in person and spend some time working through why they came up with a certain concept, then embrace that idea. Give them the time they need to justify what they have done. Whether you like it or not can be easily worked out later, but if there are parts to what they have done that have involved a lot of thought and consideration, it's best if you know what they are and give them the opportunity to explain it. You have to remember that design is something you see in an instant that often has had hours or days or more poured into it without you seeing it.

Depending on where you are in your business, you might find yourself in the position of having to justify designs internally or externally, so it's a good practice to have.

There's also plenty of room for a bit of underlying meaning if your design satisfies the minimum requirement of looking sexy. If it looks sexy, and your designer can take you through the story of how it came about, how much thought went into it, what various elements symbolize, etc., it will only make it better. These facts might pop up in stories told about the product down the track.

It's also a great way to find out whether or not a designer has put much effort at all into your design, and it's an insight into their process. I have different designers for different projects; some delve deeply into a project and have a long process they go through, others will just visualize exactly what I ask for. Some will keep throwing shit at the wall until it sticks. A process is good, but what matters is the end result. As a business owner, it's great to know what kind of results designers can get and how they go about it. Depending on the project, you might need the exact kind of approach they take.

You'll find all of this out when you sit down with a designer and ask them to go through and justify their design.

FIND GREAT DESIGNERS

I've left this topic till close to the end for good reasons. Solving a design problem is not as simple as finding a great designer, so I didn't want you to think this is the first and most important thing you should do. But this is absolutely a critical thing you should do once you understand the rest of the complexities of design. Call me a nerd, but there is nothing like finding a designer who "gets you" and can deliver something incredible for you.

But in understanding that design is complex, you must also understand that designers are infinitely more complex.

Design can sometimes be like a marriage (think Steve Jobs and Jony Ive). If you can find this, then that's great, but often you can't and often you shouldn't. I like to work with lots of different designers, and I've found them in a whole wide range of places.

Dribbble. In the early days, I liked to go to design communities like Dribbble, which are great for going through cool designs from the world's best designers. The best designs rise to the top and provide inspiration for other designers (and business owners). I found our first designer for Black Hops through Dribbble, and it turned out that, despite it being a global community, he lived right down the street!

Instagram. Instagram has emerged as an awesome place to find designers. Great companies and entrepreneurs are happy to shout out their designers, and when they do, I follow them to see what they are up to. I found a super-talented illustrator in New Zealand via a shout-out from a famous craft brewery over there recently. We have worked on a new design that looks nothing like theirs but is totally unique for our local market.

Google. Our current core range of beers was redesigned by a company I found by finding a can I liked the design of in a bottle shop and then googling to see if they had written about their design process. Through that research, I found an article that talked about the company they worked with on the redesign. It was a small group in Los Angeles that I started talking with and ended up working with on our core range rebrand.

Upwork. This isn't normally a place I would recommend to find designers, but I have to say that about ten years ago, I looked on Upwork for designers for my web agency and found a guy who could do well-priced and high-quality templates. He lived in the Philippines, and he worked with me through my web design agency, my failed software startup, my WordPress support business, and he continues to work with us weekly at the brewery. When you find a good designer relationship, hold onto it!

Inbound. One benefit of the Compound Marketing approach is that people get to learn about what you are doing. We have had many of our preferred design-related suppliers reach out to us and ask if they can work with us. Sometimes, they'll design something and send it; sometimes, they'll just ask enough times before we give them a shot. This goes for designers, photographers, merch people—you name it. A really good chunk of the people we have worked with have proactively reached out to us. This is what happens when your brand, your story, and your content becomes meaningful to your community. Compound marketing at work.

Sharing the love

Those have been some good ways for me to find a designer, but no matter how you find your designer, it's important to hold onto the ones who are working and be prepared to move on when they're not.

Some designers don't like it if you use someone else for design. But if you become an entrepreneur that cares about design, you may not be happy to use only one designer for every project. I, for one, am not, and I prefer the model of having lots of designers.

This is perfectly fine. You are the business owner; the designer is the service provider. No matter how much they love the design, relate to it, and are defined by it, it's not theirs. It's your business, and it's up to you how it's presented. That's why it's so critical that you have a good handle on design.

Be honest with your designers and make sure your designers know how you work.

Every time I work with a designer, I demand all editable source files in native format, and once the project is over, I own all of it and can do with it what I please. This has always been the case, and I've pissed off many designers over the years with this approach, but it's 100% the right approach. It's your business, it's your brand, and if a designer wants to own it, it's a red flag. If they don't want to agree to that, then find another designer.

It's normally not about legalities, though; it's normally about what design approach works for the design problem at hand. Some people are great at fun illustration, some are great at geometric shapes, some are great at minimalism, some are great at finding meaning in things and building them into a design, and some are great at working with existing assets. I have one designer who messages me late at night proactively coming up with names and descriptions of beers that he's completely invented himself! I'll think about it for a few days, chat with Eddie and Govs, sometimes decide to brew the beer because we love the name, and all of a sudden, we have a really neatly executed beer! Most designers aren't like this but having the variety is great.

Just remember that you are the lead designer. You put the work in, understand design, own the brand, and you decide who gets to work with the brand. With a whole range of weird and wonderful inputs, you are the one who is responsible for bringing it together and making sure the customer has no clue that you had more than one person making these products. It's all a reflection of the brand.

There are plenty of awesome designers around the world who will respect that; those are the ones you need to find and hang on to.

AVOID TEMPTING BRAND KILLERS

In my early days as an entrepreneur, I fell into the online marketing crowd, or "internet marketing" as it was called back then. I won't lie; there was a hell of a lot to learn from people who sold info products online. But I hit a ceiling pretty quickly when I realized that a lot of the approaches people were using didn't sit that well with me.

Well-known marketers would swear by pop-ups on websites and affiliate links and long, badly designed, over-the-top sales pages, cheesy landing pages, false scarcity, etc. None of it sat well with me, so I didn't do any of it.

Affiliate links might make you a bit of money, but once people realize you are getting paid for promoting a product, they lose trust in your recommendations. Pop-ups might increase your email list, but they annoy people and look spammy. False scarcity might boost sales short-term, but dishonesty will harm your brand in the long-term.

If you value your brand above all else, you have a chance of building something really significant. If you chase every small win at the expense of your brand, you'll end up on a hamster wheel of non-stop product launches without ever building any long-term value in your business. Prioritizing your brand is hard. It requires patience and requires you to go against common trends and sit back and watch other people make small wins regularly.

In those days, it helped me a lot to think about what some of the world's best entrepreneurs and businesses would do. Would Tesla write a blog post filled with affiliate links and popups leading you to a $9 entry-level product and ultimately a $2,000 online summit? Of course not. Their focus is to make a great product and have a great brand. They aren't looking for quick wins. They want people to feel good when they see a Tesla, visit the Tesla website, or tune into a product launch.

Loading up on techniques that people don't like doesn't make them feel good when they think of your brand. If brand is how people feel about your company, then making them feel good is the highest priority and resisting the temptation for quick wins that will ultimately make them feel worse is key.

2

STORY

64,000 YEARS IN SECONDS

At the heart of every business is the need to influence a customer to take action and buy what the business is selling. There's only one marketing strategy that has been proven to work to influence people of every age, across every culture, since the dawn of time: storytelling.

An undeniable fact in life and in business is that stories are powerful and universal.

Stories represent structures of information that are hardwired into us complicated apes. A lot of it we might not see; we might not even notice what's happening, but they influence us because we find meaning in those structures.[18]

We are attracted to stories because we want to be in those stories. They tap into familiar emotions and themes in our own lives, and we are drawn to be part of the story.

We're bored and insecure beings. We seek meaning, and the attraction to the meaning in stories causes us to change our behavior.

In 2017, *Nature* studied a hunter-gatherer tribe in the Philippines called the Agta to look at their behavior around storytelling. They

---

[18] https://www.wired.com/2011/03/why-do-we-tell-stories/

devised an ingenious test that first asked part of the group to identify the best storytellers in the group, and second, they asked the rest of the group to play a rice resource allocation game where they could decide who (if anyone) to give the rice to.

What they found was that the more storytellers in a village, the more people gave away.[19] The study was about cooperation, but isn't it wild to think that the presence of good storytellers can lead people to give away more without any expectation of something in return? Imagine what it can do when it's someone simply exchanging money for something that they feel can bring them more value than the money (every business transaction ever).

The ability to convince someone that, if they buy a product, they will be part of something, is what the best companies have always done. They use stories to do it. This goes for major corporations down to small local businesses, who, perhaps even more powerfully, use stories often, and at times without knowing it, to drive consumer behavior. I did that myself once. More on that later, but for now, let's look at an example from a brand you know (and possibly love): Apple.

As I write this in 2020, Apple has recently become the most valuable company in the world, the first to pass $1 trillion dollars, and the first to pass $2 trillion.[20]

There was a time not that long ago that the word "trillion" was a new word to describe the debt of some of the largest nations on earth. In 2020, it's the amount of money that Apple, among a few other tech giants, are worth on their own.

A trillion sounds a lot like a million and a lot like a billion, so let's just be clear about how different those numbers are, despite how similar they sound.

Dorothy C. Morrell summed it up best in 1986 by pointing out that if you think about the number in seconds that it makes it clear just how big this number is. One million seconds is 12 days. One

---

[19]   https://www.nature.com/articles/s41467-017-02036-8

[20]   https://www.forbes.com/sites/sergeiklebnikov/2020/08/24/
apple-stock-could-surge-even-higher-following-2-trillion-valuation-m
organ-stanley-says/#2c9d56bb6eda

billion seconds is 32 years. One trillion seconds is 32,000 years. That's a hell of a difference!

Apple was not always worth two trillion dollars.

In 1981, IBM released its first personal computer.[21] It wasn't the first computer or even the first personal computer, but it was the first to gain mainstream adoption in business. It was the Ford Model T of computers. And that computer, along with others before it, was a big deal.

At the time, computers were thought of like a "Big Brother" machine that operated against the desires of people. The idea of making one of these monstrous things personal was no small feat.

Apple's first computer was built five years prior, and Apple had been the darling of the business and tech world during that time. From 1978 to 1983, Apple grew 150% each year with not much competition, but that year, IBM passed Apple in market share. IBM was exploding in growth, and its operating system was fast becoming the industry standard.[22]

In 1984, Apple introduced the Macintosh and did it with great effect, using the oldest trick in the book. Storytelling.

Apple's now-famous 1984 Super Bowl commercial used the familiar sentiment of George Orwell's novel *1984* to paint a bleak picture of how the future would look like if IBM continued its dominance.

It pitched an anonymous heroine (Apple) against "Big Brother" (IBM) in a fight to save humanity from the 1984 dystopian future. It was a powerful metaphor against the history of computers being viewed as "Big Brother" and Apple emerging as a company trying to change that perception and make them personal.[23]

In a keynote address before the first preview of the commercial, Steve Jobs said this: *"It is now 1984. It appears IBM wants it all. Apple is perceived to be the only hope to offer IBM a run for its money. Dealers initially welcoming IBM with open arms now fear an IBM-dominated*

---

21   https://www.computerhistory.org/timeline/1981/

22   https://fortune.com/1984/02/20/apple-bites-back-fortune-1984/

23   https://en.wikipedia.org/wiki/1984_(advertisement)

and controlled future. They are increasingly turning back to Apple as the only force that can ensure their future freedom. IBM wants it all and is aiming its guns on its last obstacle to industry control: Apple. Will Big Blue dominate the entire computer industry? The entire information age? Was George Orwell right about 1984?"

The ad was a commercial success at the time, helping Apple successfully launch the Macintosh (a brand that lives on as one of the most loved brands over thirty-six years later) and regain critical market share against IBM. But more importantly, it was also regarded as a major turning point in the marketing of computers. Computers were now personal. And in 2020, it's clear how far that idea has gone.

And what did it take to make that happen? Not a salesperson or a marketer.

It was the oldest trick in the book—storytelling—a 3,000-year-old story called David vs. Goliath adapted for modern times by Ridley Scott, one of the most respected storytellers of all time.[24]

And yes, you should have invested in Apple. In 1984, their market cap was around $2 billion. A lot of money; 64 years in seconds. In 2020, at $2 trillion dollars, Apple is worth over 64,000 years in seconds.

HOW TO BUILD STORYTELLING INTO YOUR BUSINESS

A lot of brands try to force stories into their business. They dream up products themed around some old tale of a famous thief or a sporting legend or a cultural reference, and they hope that the stories will connect with people. Some brands have great success with this, especially if they have very deep pockets and can pay to spread the message far and wide.

In my experience, this approach doesn't suit scrappy entrepreneurs and is more likely to fail. This approach would be like creating a crappy blog post and spending thousands of dollars on Facebook

---

[24] https://en.wikipedia.org/wiki/Ridley_Scott

ads to get traffic for it. I'd rather create a great blog post that people share organically and not spend a cent.

The same approach is possible with stories. You can try to force your way into someone else's story with bulk spend, or you can discover yourself inside an existing story for free if you know what to look for.

Now, I know the objection here, what if you aren't part of a great story? Before I deal with that sad possibility, let's see if we can find a story that works. It doesn't take much. The same story can be retold and reshared and morphed in many ways over many years; we just need to find one that works.

WHY WON'T THEY WRITE ABOUT ME?

For years, I read stories about startup companies launching and local entrepreneurs "making it," and I wondered why I could never get any press for my business. Why wouldn't they tell my story?

Almost on queue each week, I would pull up my local newspaper and notice an article about a local entrepreneur but nothing on me.

In the years since, this hasn't changed. Just today, I read an article on news.com.au about a local entrepreneur named Luke. This article would be an absolute gold mine for his business. It appealed to the types of people who aspire to be his customers, it contained his business name in the title, and it has a click-baity title of "Million-Dollar Company's Secret to Success."

I read the whole thing; it was a good read. You see, Luke was down on his luck, out of work, and $100,000 in debt when he came up with an idea that was an Australian first. I know this because that last sentence you just read was the bolded subtitle of the article[25].

Luke almost failed university and was left with a $100,000 debt. He had no job prospects or direction. He wasn't a good student and had pinned his hopes on getting good grades and a well-paying job.

---

[25]   https://www.news.com.au/finance/work/careers/
social-media-mansion-milliondollar-companys-secret-to-success/news-story/5a
552ac396a92f76e3a8fe5cecc0e68b

With poor grades, this plan looked flawed, and he began applying for job after job, getting knocked back over eighty times, even from the most demeaning professions. He got a job as a valet and was looked down upon by successful people with nice cars (which he desperately wanted to be). He was at rock bottom and had to make a change.

With spare change, he built a prototype for some software to help companies market on social media. Under the wing of an inspirational mentor, Luke continued to build the product, and it grew into a multi-million-dollar business. He quit his job and joined the elite he so desperately wanted to be part of. It was an inspiring moment.

But he wasn't completely fulfilled; he felt a void and found money didn't lead to happiness. He lost his passion and his motivation, and despite buying a Lamborghini, he felt empty inside.

He changed up his game, moved away from material possessions, and instead bought his mum a Merc (yes, I noticed the inconsistency there). He became passionate about charity work. It was at that point that he returned, the hero of his own story and an inspiration for the rest of us.

Over the years, reading stories like Luke's, I noticed that almost every week there would be a similar story, and it was almost identical.

In fact, a quick glance at his story includes links to related stories.

Title: Fired at 22 to $47m a year
Subtitle: Brett was broke and down on his luck after losing his "dream job." But it was the best thing that ever happened to him.

Title: 33yo's amazing Million-Dollar Coles Deal
Subtitle: Kate started her business as a "side hustle" – but now, her products have landed in every Coles supermarket in the country.

Title: Single Mum's Hobby now $125k business
Subtitle: Briony Goldsmith thought her interests might be "a bit woo-woo" – but she ended up transforming them into a lucrative, booming business.

This isn't some spamming internet marketing blog; this is Australia's biggest news site, visited by a quarter of the population every month.[26]

Why were all these people getting free press for their stories? I mean, they are basically all the same story.

TYPES OF STORIES

We've already gone through a few story options, David vs. Goliath, the Cinderella-style comeback, etc. But there must be thousands of types of stories we could consider, right? Think about all the movies you've seen, all the books you've read, the nursery rhymes, the business stories—it's endless.

Actually, the majority of well-told stories are almost all the same story. Guy Ritchie, the famed Hollywood director, said this when discussing storytelling on the Joe Rogan podcast. Using the prodigal son as an example, he explained that all stories come back to a person having to "leave themselves," make a few mistakes, and lose some things before finally returning to realize that they were enough the whole time. He said, *The essence of narrative is only about this dynamic; there is nothing else in a story other than this dynamic."*

What he's referring to is "the hero's journey," a storytelling structure made popular in 1949 by Joseph Campbell.

> *"A hero ventures forth from the world of common day into a region of supernatural wonder: fabulous forces are there encountered and a decisive victory is won: the hero comes back from this mysterious adventure with the power to bestow boons on his fellow man."*

---

26 http://www.roymorgan.com/findings/7595-top-20-news-websites-march-2018-201805240521#:~:text=Australia's%20most%20popular%20news%20website,just%20over%205%20million%20visitors.

There are three parts:

1. The Departure Act: the Hero leaves the ordinary world

2. The Initiation Act: the Hero ventures into unknown territory (the "special world") and is transformed into a true champion through various trials and challenges

3. The Return Act: the Hero returns in triumph

Think about some of your favorite movies, *Harry Potter*, *The Matrix*, *Lord of the Rings*, *Star Wars*—every Pixar movie ever! All the same.

Neo is minding his own business, making chump change as a computer hacker in his ordinary world. Based on a feeling and an invitation from a mysterious hacker called Trinity, he decides to enter into a new world. He finds a wise guide in Morpheus, who tells him that he is "the one" and teaches him the ropes in the new world.

Things are looking okay until a true test of evil. While fighting the all-powerful agents, he is double-crossed by someone he thought was his friend, and he fails. He actually dies. But thankfully for us viewers, he makes a miraculous comeback with some help with some love from Trinity. He returns as a new person, one infinitely more powerful and with enough belief to destroy the agents who were previously thought of as indestructible.

In reality, he was the same person the whole time, but he needed the journey, the guide, and in this story, the love, to return and discover who he was.

The story I told above about my business is a simplified and imperfect version of the same thing. I was working in a great stable job (the ordinary world). Something drove me, a feeling, to quit the job and venture into a new unknown world of business where I had no experience and all the ambition to make it. But it turned out it wasn't as easy as I thought. After seven years, I was broke, had no business, was losing money each month, and couldn't see a way forward. I reached the point where I was already applying for jobs, hoping to give up and return to my ordinary world. Then, I launched one more business, which miraculously worked, and I returned as the hero of my own story.

Imagine how good it would be if I had a wise guide and a hot love interest in there!

There are many variations of the hero's journey and many layers to it. Like anything, the more you dig into storytelling, the more there is to know. If you want to write the next *Game of Thrones*, you'll need to know more than the hero's journey.

Even writing a basic, entry-level novel that anyone would finish reading requires an enormous amount of structure. You need to consider the structure (mini-plot, arch plot, etc.), the style (drama, comedy, etc.) and possible sub-styles, how far we are suspending the reader from reality (fantasy, factualism, etc.), is it a short time/long time, etc., what's the content and sub-content, where it happens, why it happens, who the main characters are, what are the main compulsory scenes, the change curve in the story, and the list goes on and on and on.[27]

As business owners, we are lucky. We don't have to write the next *Lord of the Rings*; we just have to tell a very basic story, which is almost always the same story: the hero's journey or some version of it. We can break it down a little bit further, but that basic overarching structure is enough for all of our stories.

In his book *The Seven Basic Plots: Why We Tell Stories*, Christopher Booker contends that any story will only ever consist of one, or a combination, of seven basic plots following one overall metaplot.

> *"The metaplot begins with the anticipation stage, in which the hero is called to the adventure to come. This is followed by a dream stage, in which the adventure begins, the hero has some success, and has an illusion of invincibility. However, this is then followed by a frustration stage, in which the hero has his first confrontation with the enemy, and the illusion of invincibility is lost. This worsens in the nightmare stage, which is the climax of the plot, where hope is apparently lost. Finally, in the resolution, the hero overcomes his burden against the odds."*

---

[27] https://storygrid.com/books/

Sound familiar? The hero's journey.

Booker breaks it down further into seven specific plots that represent various variations of this meta plot: overcoming the monster, rags-to-riches, the quest, voyage, and return, comedy, tragedy, and re-birth.[28] I think a few of these are particularly powerful for businesses, especially small businesses.

- The Quest - The protagonist and companions set out to acquire an important object or to get to a location. They face temptations and other obstacles along the way. My income reports were an example of this, month after month of different obstacles coming up and not getting anywhere. There's been a big trend toward this in recent years with companies like Buffer, Gimlet, ConvertKit, and many more, documenting their story day by day as they go through the ups and downs of business. It's engaging to follow along, which makes it great marketing.

- Overcoming the monster - The hero sets out to defeat an antagonistic force that threatens their homeland. Think 1984 by Apple.

- Rags to riches - The poor protagonist acquires power, wealth, and/or a mate, loses it all and gains it back, growing as a person as a result. A lot of famous businesses and entrepreneurs draw on this storyline to spread their message (Howard Shultz, Oprah, Richard Branson, or Ray Kroc, as portrayed in the movie *The Founder*). And who could forget Luke from news.com.au.

- Rebirth - An event forces the main character to change their ways and often become a better individual. *Groundhog Day*, *Beauty and the Beast*, *The Matrix*, etc. In business, an example is Steve Jobs being fired by Apple, and after experiencing a lot of hard, failing years, triumphantly returns to take Apple to become the most valuable company on earth. After getting

---

[28] https://en.wikipedia.org/wiki/The_Seven_Basic_Plots

fired from PayPal, Elon Musk returns to revolutionize space travel and the automotive industry (and be the godfather of dank memes).

This is where you need to think about your own business, your products, and your marketing to see if it matches any of these stories. There are many options for types of stories in business, and the three that stand out are:

1. Founding stories

2. Customer stories

3. Product stories

FOUNDING STORIES

Founding stories are very powerful for a business. Everyone loves a good story about how a company is started, and in many cases, those stories will live on in the culture of the organization, it's products, and it's brand for as long as the company exists.

The Quest

The protagonist and companions set out to acquire an important object or to get to a location.

Just before selling my business WP Curve to GoDaddy in 2016, one conversation at a pub would once again put me smack bang in the middle of another great story. This time, however, I was able to realize it and capitalize on it.

As me and my two mates Eddie and Govs sat around a bar table and discussed craft beer, Eddie asked Govs a question: "Do you reckon a stout with eggnog characteristics would work? Not sweet and sickly but a dry stout with subtle characteristics of what you find in eggnog: brandy, cinnamon, nutmeg, and vanilla."

He continued. "I reckon this is a cool beer idea, and I submitted to another beer competition with a brewery called 4 Pines when they were looking for beer ideas. It didn't win, but they said they liked the idea, and they sent me a carton of beer as a consolation prize."

That wasn't enough for Eddie; he wanted to make the beer.

Just about every bloke I know has found themselves in this position, sitting around having a beer, pitching an idea that would ultimately never get followed up on. That's why a lot of people can relate to our story and find meaning in what happened next.

Because we did follow up on the idea.

Govs agreed it was a cool beer concept, and two weeks later, we were back in the same spot, brewing the Eggnog Stout, thus beginning our quest to leave the ordinary world and enter into a brave new world, a world of every bloke's dreams, a world where you can make beer, drink beer, and get paid for it.

Six years on, we are one of Australia's fastest-growing companies, and up there with some of the most recognized independent beer brands. The business is doubling every year and is well over ten times larger than my last business WP Curve. There's been a hell of a lot of ups and downs on this quest, and we've brought our audience along with us every step of the way. From day one, this has been virtually the only marketing we have done.

You know what's especially cool? I'm currently finalizing this section in this book, drinking an Eggnog Stout I just bought from a bottle shop within walking distance of my house. They stock it because the bottle shop is owned by the largest alcohol retailer in Australia, who now stocks Eggnog Stout.

Overcoming the monster

The hero sets out to defeat an antagonistic force which threatens their homeland.

Overcoming the monster is a great plot for business owners, particularly disruptive startups. You encourage your customers to back you in a noble quest to free them from another monstrous company (your competitor). Like David vs. Goliath or 1984 by Apple.

The key is not to present yourself as the victim. I see a lot of this sentiment in the business world where small business owners complain about the power of larger businesses. Stories are supposed to inspire, and no one aspires to be a victim.

Don't think about a small, powerless David who theoretically has no chance against the all-powerful (and hopefully, evil) Goliath. Think about someone who others see as incapable in an impossible fight but who believes themselves that they can do it, and fundamentally they do have greatness within them. Perhaps they are the only person who thinks they can do it. That's a hero. Everyone wants to be that person.

In Australia, everyone used to continuously complain about the power of the lobbying organizations involved in taxi services. Everyone hated the taxi service, and there were lots of companies who started with the story of "Taxis have too much power, so back us." And you know what? It's not inspiring.

Taxis were the enemy. I hated them; they were the closest thing to a real, live monster I could think of. The service was awful. You'd line up for hours trying to get one. People were being assaulted in taxi lines regularly. Often, you just wouldn't go out because you knew it would be impossible to get home. Calling the company did nothing because they wouldn't come if you called them. The drivers were rarely nice, they drove like arseholes, and the cars smelled like shit. If you had a bad experience in a taxi, you couldn't click a button to give feedback and get your money back. You had to suck it up because that was the experience.

Meanwhile, overseas, Uber was taking off as a pretty decent alternative. Drivers who have accountability and clean cars, and you can click a button on an app, and it comes to you? Sign me up!

Uber eventually came to Australia and changed the game. They made some mistakes for sure, stretched a few laws here and there, but ultimately, they gave customers a far better service and a level of control and convenience they desperately wanted. A company that started only a few years prior had accomplished something that no local company had for decades prior. It's a great story.

Many disruptive startups, whether deliberate or otherwise, follow this same trajectory. Elon doubled down on Tesla Motors because he noticed the major car companies were doing nothing in the electric car space. They were making all of us customers complicit in destroying the environment, while the technology existed to innovate and move toward much more sustainable transport. Tesla, which started in a small garage, rebuilding Lotus cars into electric vehicles, prevailed against a monstrous industry destroying the planet. That's a story!

Netflix brought a level of convenience and quality for entertainment that people had been craving for decades. In the process, they finished Blockbuster, a tired company that everyone knew for punishing them with late fees and offering the same thing year after year after year.

Bitcoin and blockchain-based companies are doing the same thing right now to tired evil banking companies that have overstayed their welcome.

People love these stories, they want to be part of it, and they want to back these companies.

Rags to riches

The poor protagonist acquires power, wealth, and/or a mate, loses it all, and gains it back, growing as a person as a result.

What's brilliant about rags-to-riches stories is that humans have a way of generally not feeling like they are enough. No matter what they have, they want more. Of course, a rags-to-riches story will inspire someone who has nothing, but it will also inspire someone who has everything but still wants more. Rags-to-riches is about someone overcoming all odds to get more. It's universal and works at every scale.

The movie *The Founder* tracks Ray Kroc in his quest to found one of the most valuable brands to ever exist, McDonald's. Ray is a traveling salesman in the 1950s, a bit dorky, but a good, hardworking, and ambitious man. He wants more. He's not happy with his ordinary world.

He sees an opportunity in drive-in restaurants being run inefficiently and hears about two brothers doing something different in another state. He convinces the owners to have him lead their effort to franchise the business. Through a lot of ups and downs (mostly downs), he ends up buying out the brothers and building what we know today as McDonald's.

Many entrepreneurs of our generation have built their empire off similar stories. Oprah Winfrey, Tony Robbins, Richard Branson, Elon Musk, Mark Cuban, Andrew Carnegie, Henry Ford, and the list goes on.

Amazon started in Jeff Bezos' garage. Apple started in Steve Jobs' family's garage. Black Hops Brewing starting in Govs' garage. Yes, my point is that Black Hops is basically the same as Apple and Amazon, a point I regularlymake to our investors.

People love a good rags-to-riches story.

Rebirth

An event forces the main character to change their ways and often become a better individual.

Rebirth has become a very powerful way for modern businesses to tell their story, and there seems to be no end to the bad things people will accept from someone as long as good things follow. It's a bit of a disturbing trend, but it's a marketing goldmine for the right story.

A lot of businesses start because of some kind of rebirth, and people like it. Get on Instagram, and you won't have to scroll far to find a fitness influencer who's given up a lazy life after discovering a revolutionary diet, supplement, treatment, or workout to start a brand-new, much-improved life.

Steve Jobs had to be fired by Apple to be reborn and return to save the company (a rebirth of its own).

Every reformed addict or sinner who becomes good inspires us because we realize we could be on either side of that equation.

If your business came about because of a drastic change in you or in your market, then you have your founding story ready to go. And if you don't think it did, then maybe look a bit more carefully because it probably did.

Founding stories can be used in any number of ways, which I'll run through in "How to tell your story." But founding stories aren't the only stories that businesses can tell.

CUSTOMER STORIES

Some of the most powerfully motivating stories for a business are customer stories. You don't have to go too far to find customer stories: before and after photos for fitness businesses, the Subway guy, customers' adventures using Patagonia gear, and just about every SAAS company you can think of.

For fun, I'll open up the websites of the first three SAAS companies I think of based on apps I use:

- The Slack homepage has a story of a well-known company, Intuit, using the service to accomplish goals quicker.

- Pipedrive contains videos of customers telling their stories about how Pipedrive enabled them to sell more.

- The Xero homepage contains links to stories from customers who use Xero and who are "making the world a more beautiful place."

I'm not sure at what point accounting became beautiful, but I'm down for a good yarn!

Customer stories are powerful because they stop you from talking about yourself. A big trap in storytelling is to talk about yourself too much to the point where it all becomes a little bit self-centered, and you lose people. You can tell as many customer stories as you want, and you won't lose people (unless it's boring and the exact same story over and over with the same characters).

Customers can be on their own quest. Maybe they had been existing and struggling for many years before discovering your product and your product becomes the important object in their quest.

Customers can overcome monsters. They could use your product to defeat an antagonistic force threatening their livelihood.

Customers can use your product or service to go from rags to riches.

If you want to escape the trap of talking about yourself too much, then customer stories are a great way to do that.

Testimonials framework

Consider this simple framework for getting testimonials from customers. Well-written testimonials on sales pages sell; however, customers will never provide testimonials in a well-written manner without prompting. Customers will be honest and raw, which is great, but to truly capture the story and enable you to present it in a way that will change behavior, you have to ask the right questions.

Here is a very quick framework you can use for asking for a testimonial. Keep in mind that, depending on what field you are in, only some of this might be relevant. I've had businesses across software, services, products, and now, beer. Use the bits that work to help you craft a good story.

Just so we have an example to work with, let's say you sell software that helps make beer delivery easier. Currently, we don't use any software for this, and we do 600+ deliveries a month, so we are ripe to be sold a beer delivery software app. Let's imagine there's a beer delivery software company called Keg Send. They have a good solution for delivering beer, and they want to convince us to sign up as a customer. How would they use customer testimonials to get this done?

Here are the questions to ask someone when you want a testimonial. And yes, some of these are awkward questions to ask, but the deeper you dig, the more likely you are to find something valuable. If you don't feel comfortable asking all of these, that's fine, just ask your normal questions and look for these themes in the responses, then structure your testimonial or customer story that way. If you are comfortable asking for the full story, here is the framework:

1. The Departure Act: the Hero leaves the ordinary world

If you consider that we are writing this story for someone who's close to signing up for this app, we have to place them into the story where they are currently at. They have probably thought about signing up, but they aren't sure if they are suitable. This act is designed to help them understand that they have a lot in common with the hero of this story.

Question: For a long time, you got by without software like Keg Send. Describe what that time was like.

Example answer: We were a fast-growing brewery, and while we had issues with delivery, we had issues with everything, so it was just one of a long list of issues to deal with. Once we started doing over twenty deliveries a day per driver, the cracks were starting to show. Drivers were stressed, the back-office team didn't know when or if beers were delivered, customers would call up unhappy, and when there was an issue, there was no way to trace it back to work out what happened. In short, we were not confident that if a customer ordered beer that they would get the beer. As a company that's in the business of making beer, that is a big problem.

Question: There must have been a reason why you didn't sign up earlier. What was that reason?

Example answer: We were very busy dealing with all the things that you have to deal with as a high-growth brewery. We are often sold solutions to things, but when we try them out, they just waste more of our extremely limited time. We were skeptical about whether Keg Send would actually help and whether it would mean customers who ordered beer would actually get the beer flawlessly every time.

Question: What was the thing that triggered you to sign up?

Example answer: There was one day on Friday afternoon in a week during a limited release. We'd had a record week, the sales team was celebrating, and everyone was stoked. We got a call from one of our best customers saying they hadn't got their delivery, and they had people coming into the store who couldn't get their beer. It was too late to get the beer out that day, and we couldn't work out what had happened. It turned an awesome day into a bit of a bummer.

2. The Initiation Act: the Hero ventures into unknown territory (the "special world") and is transformed into a true champion through various trials and challenges.

Some of these questions can be painful to ask, but there are two reasons to delve into these. First, if you can capture these elements in your customer story, it becomes a much better story. Second, if you can show a potential customer that signing up will be well worthwhile but not easy, it puts them firmly in the hero's journey. It's easy to sign up for something that has no risks, but signing up for something where risks are present, well, that's an opportunity to shine!

Question: *What were some of the original stumbling blocks when using Keg Send?*

Example answer: *We had never used software to help us deliver beer before, so it was a big change for the drivers. At the start, drivers wouldn't use it until the end of the day, and then they'd update everything in the app. It was good that they updated it at the end of the day, but it didn't solve the problem of not knowing what was going on during the day.*

Question: *What did you initially hate about using Keg Send?*

Example answer: *The back-office team liked the idea of the software, but it didn't make sense if drivers weren't using it properly. We were back at square one with no data until the end of the day.*

Question: *Was there a time when using Keg Send where you thought you'd made the wrong decision?*

Example answer: *After a week or two, all we heard were complaints from drivers about having to use an app for every delivery and from the back office for not having the information they needed. We wondered if it would just be easier to go back to having no app for deliveries.*

Question: *How did you fix the situation and make Keg Send the right decision? What exactly did you do?*

Example answer: *After the first week, when the drivers struggled, we started applauding drivers who came back to the brewery with all their deliveries signed off. The drivers loved it, and the ones who didn't get the applause quickly understood why. Seems childish, but getting this working was a big thing, and this was a fun way to get everyone on board.*

3. The Return Act: The Hero returns in triumph.

This is the important part where you paint your customer as the hero.

Question: *What action did you take to ensure Keg Send worked?*

Example answer: *After two weeks, we called all of the drivers together and explained the importance of taking this seriously. We told them the story of the customer being upset and having it ruin the day for lots of people and showed them how powerful and important the simple act of delivering beer on time could be.*

Question: *Tell me when you first realized Keg Send worked.*

Example answer: *The next week, we got a call from a customer complaining about how they hadn't got their delivery. This had happened countless times before, and every time we'd had to explain we didn't know when it would arrive, but it would be there today. This day was different. We checked Keg Send, and it showed that the driver had completed her most recent delivery six km down the road only eight minutes earlier and was due to arrive in four minutes. The customer was stoked to have this level of detail and put extra effort into promoting the beer. The beer rocked and was all sold out that night.*

Question: *How did your colleagues feel about this new situation?*

Example answer: *Everyone was happy. It was great to get a call like this and give them a real answer and then make them happy with timely delivery.*

Question: *How did the higher-ups feel about this new situation?*

Example answer: *Managers often hear about deliveries gone bad, so they were stoked not to hear these stories but instead hear a story about a customer who called up, was surprised by how much we knew about the delivery and ended up getting their beer only five minutes later.*

Question: *How did Keg Send solve your original problem?*

Example answer: *Originally, we had a lot of unhappy customers, and our staff couldn't do anything to make them happy. Once we committed to properly implementing Keg Send, we know exactly where our beer is so we can delight our customers every time they call, and the team is a lot less anxious.*

By the way, I made up this app called Keg Send; no such app exists as far as I know. But it sounds kind of dreamy, right?

There is an enormous amount of power in this one single testimonial. From here, you can write a whole customer story and use this as a base for any kind of marketing you plan on delivering from blog posts to direct response copy to videos, social media—the whole lot. And of course, you can go back and get more information on the things that could add to your story.

Here are a few examples you can build from this one testimonial.

Slogan: Perfect delivery of the world's most precious resource—beer.
Usage: Everywhere from your physical product to a headline for ads to your website headline to news stories, etc.

Service description: Keg Send removes the confusion around beer delivery and lets you, the brewer, deliver your beer to the right customer, on time, as planned.
Usage: Website first description, brochures, Google ads, conference signs, etc.

Long customer hero story:

Usage: Company website, every press opportunity, speaking at events, sales rep in-store visit cheat sheets, brochures, corporate induction manuals, etc.

"Keg Send has one goal: perfect delivery of the world's most precious resource—beer.

Kaitlin was a delivery driver for 3 Trees Brewing. 3 Trees was exploding in growth, and every problem was a big problem! It took a while to realize, but once 3 Trees was delivering over twenty beers a day, cracks in the delivery process were showing, and customers were beginning to distrust the brand. Kaitlin felt every bit of that pain.

3 Trees was so busy that, until that point, they hadn't stopped to consider how to do things better.

One Friday in May, going into a difficult time of the year, the team was riding high after a record week of deliveries. It was then that one of Kaitlin's stops, Craig, called up the head office. Craig, one of 3 Trees' best customers on the Sunshine Coast, was furious. He had people turning up all day looking for the beer and still hadn't received his delivery. He'd called and couldn't get any information on when the delivery would arrive. Where the fuck was his normal driver, Kaitlin!

Kaitlin ended up making the delivery, but not before the whole team was de-railed by the negative feedback. Kaitlin wasn't happy about it, and this was the straw that broke the camel's back. She told the owners this wasn't good enough, and she would find a solution.

She came across Keg Send and co-ordinated with the office to do a trial run. This would be a big change for the drivers. They would now have to check into every delivery and use a new app for scheduling their runs. Not fun.

The back-office team loved the idea of knowing exactly where deliveries were, but the drivers weren't convinced. It was just more work.

But Kaitlin had a friend in Ryan. Ryan embraced the idea, and he loved knowing that, when he did a good job, it would be recognized. He loved the fact that he could tick his jobs off as they were done, and his customers were well-looked-after by the back office.

On the trial day, Kaitlin and Ryan returned to the brewery five minutes apart, and the back-office team greeted them with a standing ovation. All the deliveries were made and checked off, the customers were happy, and it was easy.

While no other drivers received rounds of applause that day, they would shortly.

Kaitlin, the humble delivery driver, had changed the game.

Short customer hero story:

Usage: Different parts of company website, staff inductions, customer scripts, social media, cheat sheets, etc.

"Deliveries used to be very confusing; missed drops, confused customers, and refunds were all normal—until Katilin decided enough was enough. She convinced the team to use an app to track the drivers and get them to enter their deliveries. We started using Keg Send, and from that point on, customers were happy, managers were happy, and beer was getting delivered on schedule."

These stories have enormous currency, and there's no limit to how and where you can apply them. Once you have a good handle on why someone would use your product or service, the opportunities are endless. Podcasts, Instagram photos, press stories, ads—you name it, you can do it now. You have a great story that can be told in many ways.

And by the way, if you do have this magical product called Keg Send, please let me know because we need it!

PRODUCT STORIES

The formation of your business isn't the only story event worth thinking about. Every product is a formation of something new and, therefore, a ripe target for a story. In some cases, products are so well known that the business behind the product takes a back seat.

Your product might be the hero, or your product might enable your customers to be the hero. Or your product might be engaged in a war against a formidable opponent. Your product might even be a villain because you have a new product coming out that's the hero.

Every time we release a beer at Black Hops, we try to think about whether there's a story behind how the beer came about. In fact, the story could exist before the beer exists, and that can work too.

Eggnog Stout - Our original Eggnog Stout is part of our founding story. My business partner Eddie had a great idea for a beer, offered it up to another brewery that rejected it, and so we made it ourselves to much fanfare, enabling him to leave his boring corporate job and embark on a quest for beer glory.

Pale Ale - Things didn't always go to plan at Black Hops. In fact, the first year was a real struggle. While we were making some great beers, we hadn't quite captured the heart and soul of our drinkers. Each year, there was a countdown of the best Australian craft beers. I thought 2016 was our year, and after finishing 113th the year before, our bottled Beach House Saison style beer would be high up the list. As I listened to every beer announced from 100 to 1, I gradually realized that, once again, we would not make the list. On Monday, I messaged Eddie and Govs and said we needed to talk about a new core range beer. I proposed that our first beer in cans wouldn't be Beach House but would be a new beer. It would not be something creative and cool like Beach House but something extremely simple, a pale ale, the Black Hops Beer for every occasion. We would even call it Pale Ale so every person who walked into a bottle shop knew exactly what it was.

A month later, we cracked the first-ever Black Hops can, Black Hops Pale Ale, and the following year, as they counted down the Hottest 100 craft beers, we gathered in celebration with the team as they announced Black Hops Pale Ale at #20, the highest debut entry for that year. Pale Ale had become our best seller, our most popular beer, and had catapulted us into an era of growth that hasn't slowed down in the years since.

G.O.A.T. - In 2018, a new style of beer was emerging in Australia, referred to as a New England IPA (NEIPA) or Hazy IPA. It had attracted so much fanfare that it was added to the official style guidelines for Australia's most prestigious beer awards, the AIBAs.

We hadn't brewed a beer of this style before, and we decided to brew our first one specifically for these awards. With tongue in cheek, we debated a fun name that we hoped would be shown on the screen on the night as they read out the gold medals. We were close to calling it "AIBA Gold" but decided to wind back the obnoxiousness just a little bit and call it G.O.A.T. (Greatest Of All Time). We headed to Melbourne for the awards and with great expectation as they read out the gold medals for the NEIPA category, and in big shining lights, we saw "Black Hops G.O.A.T." on the screen.

In those stories, the beer is the hero, but that doesn't have to be the case.

Pina Colada - A few weeks leading up to the biggest beer festival of the year (GABS), we had a post in the Black Hops Ambassador Facebook Group about how some of our audience might put forward a beer idea. We replied and said, do it here and now, what's on your mind? Marc, from our group, suggested a hazy nitro IPA with pineapple and coconut in the tradition of a Pina Colada. We loved the idea and joked that this could become our festival beer that year. As it turned out, the festival was canceled a few weeks later due to the COVID-19 pandemic, and the thread died off. But we decided it would be a great idea to make the beer anyway, and we made it secretly and released it despite no festival happening. We championed Marc as the originator of the idea and told the story of how it came about. Marc was the hero who saved GABS.

I know these are just beer releases, and you might be working on something, let's say, a lot more meaningful, but the fact is that stories are universal and can scale infinitely. If it works for a small-batch beer release, it will work for whatever product you are planning on launching.

By the way, none of these stories happen in some kind of dishonest way. These are all legitimate stories.

Product stories are particularly powerful if you are launching something new. If you can position your product as the hero to drag your customer out of the darkness, it can be especially effective. New companies that do well; they tell a great story about how their products can be the change you need.

- Uber heroically saved you from dirty Falcons and drunken fights in taxi ranks (at least if you're Australian). Uber's original slogan in 2010: Everyone's Private Driver[29].

- Canva heroically liberates you from the control of snobby designers and enables you to create on your own. Original slogan: Design For Everyone.[30]

- Airbnb freed you from shitty hotels that smelled like piss and charged you a small fortune. In 2007, AirBed & Breakfast had a childish, bubbly-looking, pink and blue website with the slogan "AirBed & Breakfast is the fun, affordable alternative to hotels for your favorite events." The following year, the cartoons were gone, and the slogan was "Forget Hotels." The hero was emerging. Or more importantly, the villain was made very clear.

- We follow SpaceX because their mission is to colonize Mars and free us from the stench we've created here on earth. Rockets were always cool, but as we continue to fuck earth up more and more, and Elon edges closer and closer to his goal of colonizing another planet, we eat up this new idea more and more.[31]

Humans are in a constant, desperate search for a hero. If you can position your product as that hero, it's marketing dynamite.

IMPROVING YOUR STORY WITH A VILLAIN

We already have a protagonist in your story, i.e., you, or your company, or your product, or your customer. But who's the enemy?

Picking an enemy can make a story very spicy. Donald Miller, in *Building a Storybrand*, says, *"What is the chief source of conflict that your*

---

[29] https://www.businessinsider.com/ubers-design-history-2010-2016-2016-2?r=AU&IR=T

[30] https://uxtimeline.com/canva.html

[31] https://www.spacex.com/human-spaceflight/mars/

products and services defeat? Talk about this villain. The more you talk about the villain, the more people will want a tool to help them defeat the villain."[32] If there is an obvious direct villain that your product aims to defeat, then you are in luck (like taxis for Uber or hotels for Airbnb). But even if there's not, there are still ways of going about it. Perhaps there's one that's adjacent to the main story.

A $24M MARKETING GIFT

At the time of writing this, I'm watching an exquisite example of this play out right before my eyes. Jason Fried and David Heinemeier Hansson (DHH) became well-known for one of the first cloud-based project management tools, Basecamp. In the years since, they have stayed a constant in the online entrepreneur and software startup space, in no small way due to their contrarian views.

In the last few weeks, they rolled out the launch of a new email software called HEY. It's exceptionally ambitious even with their platform to build a new email tool, but the storytelling at the heart of their marketing for HEY is on point, and it's worth digging into.

HEY is the hero. Email hasn't changed in sixteen years, and the existing companies have given up on servicing their customers. Jason and DHH think it can be done better.

Or maybe Email is the hero; it's just been led astray. That sometimes happens on the hero's journey. They describe HEY as their "love letter to Email."

In any case, it's a great story with at least one hero and all the necessary spicy bits.

They begin their journey by finding the perfect domain name and building out a solution that's fundamentally different from what's currently available.

It hasn't been easy because there are many big players involved, and none of them want a new entrant.

The idea itself focuses on privacy and puts the likes of Facebook and Google as clear antagonists. The marketing up to the launch

---

[32]   https://www.amazon.com/dp/B06XFJ2JGR?ref_=k4w_ss_details_rh

focuses heavily on intrusive tracking pixels and the unethical practice of large companies selling personal data. Their heroic product Hey solves all of this, well, for email at least.

About the only major tech player who isn't an enemy of these guys is Apple. That is, until launch week when the story gets really juicy. This week, Apple rejected their app on the basis that HEY wasn't abiding by their revenue-sharing agreements.

When this happened, all hell broke loose. Jason and DHH went after Apple hard on Twitter. DHH tweeted:

"Wow. I'm literally stunned. Apple just doubled down on their rejection of HEY's ability to provide bug fixes and new features, unless we submit to their outrageous demand of 15-30% of our revenue. Even worse: We're told that unless we comply, they'll REMOVE THE APP.[33]"

The story ended up on major podcasts like Recode Decode, major news platforms like Yahoo Finance, and *The New York Times* as the founders doubled down on their stance, referring to Apple as gangsters.[34]

The fun thing is that anyone who's ever submitted an app to the App Store knows it's probably going to be rejected. Dealing with Apple is notoriously painful. You also know they are going to make you opt-in to their revenue-share agreements. This is very normal, and I dare say Jason and DHH would have known exactly that would happen. But they also knew that they have hundreds of thousands of developers in their audience who also feel this pain but don't have a big enough voice to be heard.

Jason and DHH were certainly heard, and it resulted in an obscene amount of free attention to their new product. In the weeks after launch, it was impossible not to know about HEY. In the first two weeks of launch, 120,000 people joined the waiting list or got an invite code from a friend and signed up for a HEY account. This was before it was made available to the public. That's a staggering number.

---

[33]   https://twitter.com/dhh/status/1272968382329942017

[34]   https://twitter.com/SquawkAlley/status/1273652569374687232

Imagine how much you would have to spend to get 120,000 people desperately waiting to try your new software app. Consider that there are already thousands of great email apps from the best software companies in the world with years of development in them already. Considering that no one really wants to leave their existing email app, it's a pain in the arse to do so, which means no one is really looking for a better email app. But let's say enough people are, and let's do some dodgy napkin math to work out how much it would cost to get them to try yours.

Say you signed up for Google Ads and bought clicks for keywords like "email software" or "better email software" or "simpler email platform." Say the clicks cost you $7 per click, and once they got to your page, you converted them at 5% to an opt-in for the waiting list. Let's say from there that you convert 70% of those on the waiting list to actual trial users. That's $200 per user.

To get 120,000 people using the software, it would cost you $24,000,000.

Sure, some of these numbers might be off, but it shows how impossibly difficult it is to gain and maintain people's attention to things like this.

Jason and DHH did it with a few tweets and a couple of podcast interviews. And of course, the impressive brand they've built over decades in the industry (compounding at work).

If you think I'm cynical for thinking this was deliberate, consider this quote from a best-selling book that they wrote called Rework.[35]

"Pick a fight

If you think a competitor sucks, say so. When you do that, you'll find that others who agree with you will rally to your side. Being the anti-_____ is a great way to differentiate yourself and attract followers......Having an enemy gives you a great story to tell customers, too. Taking a stand always stands out. People get stoked by conflict. They take sides. Passions are ignited. And that's a good way to get people to take notice."

---

[35] https://www.amazon.com.au/Rework-Jason-Fried/dp/0307463745

I mentioned their tweets above; they aren't just screaming about how bad Apple is. Jason and David have been sharing tweets all week about how much people love HEY. But not just any tweets; rarely do they share tweets that say, "HEY is great; it's so easy to use."

Most of the shared tweets specifically mention the villain or the parts of the story that make HEY heroic.

@DonMacAskill *"HEY...is incredible. Using it feels so warm & human, focused on your privacy (no spy pixels!), and re-imagines email to be intuitive again (The Feed and Paper Trail) Feels like 16 years ago when Gmail changed email forever."*[36]

@jtclitigation *"Just created my brand spankin' new HEY email account. Thank you for giving us an email service provider that doesn't sell our personal information and provides a calm, intuitive user experience."*[37]

Before long, we had a resolution. HEY was let into the app store, didn't have to forgo 30% in revenues, and what's more, Apple actually announced changes to some of their app store policies.[38]

What was already a decent story was now an epic David (literally) vs. Goliath battle. And David had won. What's better is that we won, too. Apple will now give developers and entrepreneurs more options for review when submitting to the App Store, making the story as much about us as it is about HEY. DHH tweeted:

"Hopefully this paves an illuminated path for approval for other multi-platform SAAS applications as well. There are still a litany of antitrust questions to answer, but things legitimately got a little better. New policies, new precedence. Apple took a great step forward."[39]

---

[36] https://twitter.com/DonMacAskill/status/1272932739222650880

[37] https://twitter.com/jtclitigation/status/1275184849935097856

[38] https://techcrunch.com/2020/06/22/apple-will-soon-let-developers-challenge-app-store-rules/

[39] https://twitter.com/dhh/status/1276158293375934470

Now is HEY going to take over email? Let's be honest, probably not; that's an exceptionally tall order. But do they have more chances than the next person who doesn't want to spend $24m on paid ads? Yes, I think so.

HOW TO TELL YOUR STORY

If you want to unlock the power of storytelling, you need to know how and when to tell your business stories. Whether it's a founding story, a customer story, or a product story, there are people out there who want to hear it.

Start planning

It's amazing to me how many people don't even think about storytelling in business. If you're being interviewed by a journalist or on a podcast, writing a product description, or trying to convince investors or the bank to give you money, then you are in the business of storytelling.

A little bit of planning wouldn't go astray! Before you next undertake any kind of marketing or PR, just pause and think about the story you are telling. I wish I thought about this back in the day when I wondered why everyone else was getting covered, and I wasn't. But it's pretty clear now that my story wasn't interesting enough. I hadn't failed badly enough, and I hadn't succeeded massively enough, or if I had, I hadn't figured out a good way to present my story in those terms.

Put a little bit of work into telling your story, and you will find a lot more success when you tell it.

Tell it as often as you can

Every time you communicate about your business or your products, you have an opportunity to tell a story. Sometimes, it feels really awkward to rehash your story. You feel like you've told it a thousand times, and no one really wants to hear it again.

I was on a podcast recently, and they asked me how Black Hops started. I thought, *Fuck, here we go again*. "Okay, so there's this dude called Eddie, he had an idea for a beer, he told a dude called Govs, blah blah blah." I spoke for ten minutes on our story until the host interrupted me and said, "I'm so sorry: I totally forgot to press record. Would you mind telling that again?" I made a joke of it and painfully told it again, albeit in a slightly different way just so I wasn't bored out of my brain.

I get it; it gets boring telling the same stories over and over again. But trust me, the chance of someone being bored hearing it, versus the likelihood of the listener being new and eating it up is very low if it's a great story. Great stories are worth telling repeatedly, and it's an important skill for a business owner.

Figure out what's interesting to others

Sometimes there are parts to a story structure that seem to be far more interesting to others than you would think. For example, when it comes to founding stories, I've found that the low point, the failure, gets an enormous amount of attention. This seems to be an emerging trend with failure almost being glorified in the startup community of late. It's like people prefer to fail than actually succeed!

But, failure has always been a gripping part of a good success story.

Thomas Edison inventing a lightbulb is pretty interesting. But the fact that he tried 10,000 different designs before one worked makes it compelling. I wonder how many times that story has been told in the last 140 years, and I wonder at what point it went from 1,000 to 3,000 to 10,000. Let's just agree it was a shitload of lightbulbs.

Colonel Sanders was turned down 1,009 times while trying to sell his fried chicken recipe. He was 65 years old when he started KFC. Reading those highlights, you'd assume he failed at least 1,000 times at this idea and failed for at least 65 years of his life leading up to KFC.

Failure stories are very relatable because everyone has experienced failure, and most people are probably experiencing some kind of failure shortly before hearing of the story. They desperately want to believe that their failure is part of a larger success story. So they place themselves into the story.

Failure might be the missing piece in the story you are trying to tell.

In the beer game, new beers are something that gets us a fair bit of attention. What might seem to be another day in the life of a brewery might seem wild to the local paper. Every time we release a weird beer, we see it as an opportunity to get some press.

Awards is another one we use in beer and one I had used many years before. In 2012, there was a competition by *Smarter Business Ideas* magazine to crown Australia's best bloggers. I was nominated in the business bloggers category, and I told all potential voters that if they voted for me, I would give them free beer. I was joking, of course. This was years before I owned a brewery, but it was a bit of fun and enough to get me voted in as Australia's top business blogger. I'm not sure it was a particularly hard-fought category, but for a few years after that, it was often mentioned in stories about me, and I was able to use it to further my interest in that world, including landing a keynote presenter spot at Australia's biggest blogger conference, Problogger.

This has not changed. There are at least three different beer awards we submit to every year, and when we do well, it's a great opportunity for press. The press loves doing stories on local companies winning awards!

In your field, it might be something different, but I'm sure there are trends you can look for that people love hearing about. It's sometimes hard to escape yourself and figure out what other people are seeing, and sometimes it feels odd to be promoting something that doesn't seem that interesting to you. But it's not about you. It's about your potential customer or supporter or sharer finding something interesting about your story. And what that is might surprise you.

Include numbers

I've noticed most business stories are filled with impressive numbers or at least numbers that are impressive to people who are seeking to place themselves inside your story.

Think about the articles from the newspaper above. One story mentioned $47m in revenue a year. The other one mentioned a

"$125k business." To some people, those numbers might not be too impressive. I'm sure Jeff Bezos, who at the time of writing is worth $147,000,000,000, isn't all that impressed with $125,000. But Susan, who's contemplating life and work after having a few kids and is thinking about starting a business, might be super-inspired about the possibility of working from home, having flexibility, and earning as much as she would in the corporate world. The numbers grab Susan's attention.

So what are the interesting numbers in your story?

WHERE TO TELL YOUR STORY

Storytelling is one of those skills that's useful in many areas. Peter Guber, an American business executive, entrepreneur, educator, filmmaker, and author, puts it this way: *"Over the years, I've learned that the ability to articulate your story or that of your company is crucial in almost every phase of enterprise management. It works all along the business food chain: A great salesperson knows how to tell a story in which the product is the hero. A successful line manager can rally the team to extraordinary efforts through a story that shows how short-term sacrifice leads to long-term success. An effective CEO uses an emotional narrative about the company's mission to attract investors and partners, to set lofty goals, and to inspire employees."*[40]

As a business owner, there are many opportunities to tell your story, some obvious, some not so obvious.

- Slogans - If you can capture your story in a few words, you can display it everywhere. Da Beers, A Diamond is Forever.[41]

- Website - Homepage copy, every product page, about page, etc. Airbnb - Forget Hotels.

---

[40] https://hbr.org/2007/12/the-four-truths-of-the-storyteller

[41] https://www.debeersgroup.com/the-group/about-debeers-group/brands/a-diamond-is-forever

- Events - Events are perfect for telling a story. Plan and structure it so that it works, and the results will be massive.

- Books - If you have a business and the opportunity is there to write a book, that's a great option. We did that with Black Hops with our book Operation Brewery, and while it's not for everyone, it's still a big point of difference for us, and every week, we sit down and sign copies to send out. It's also mentioned regularly when we talk to people about Black Hops, and that's when you know things are having an impact.[42]

- Podcasts - If you're ever invited on a podcast, this is a great platform for telling a story. I did hundreds of them early on and still say yes more often than not when I'm invited on podcasts. They are intimate and powerful and may be the best way to practice your story while undertaking valuable marketing at the same time.

- Product launches - When you next launch a product, have a think about if this product could be a hero in a story. There's a good chance it can. You've probably made it because you're unhappy with what else is available. Could this product be the hero and the existing product be the villain? Like the HEY example, the launch of the product is the time to tell that story.

- Human Resources - Anything staff-related is a great place for storytelling: induction booklets, employment ads, staff meetups, etc. Your staff are the drivers of your business, and they have to be behind the story, so don't be afraid to tell it.

- Investors - If you are like us and are regularly engaging with investors, that's another avenue to consider. From the beginning, investors have wanted to know the story of our business.

---

[42] https://www.amazon.com.au/
Operation-Brewery-step-step-building-ebook/dp/B01J4UOKMU/
ref=sr_1_1?dchild=1&keywords=operation+brewery&qid=1595750058&sr=8-1

The list could go on. Any time you are talking about your business, your product, your staff, etc., you can use storytelling.

WHAT IF THERE IS NO STORY

I often confront this question in my discussions around storytelling: What if I don't have a great story? Unfortunately, if you've read this whole chapter and still feel like you don't have a story, I don't have good news for you.

The last thing I want, however, is for you to make up some cool story to sell your products. Again, Peter Guber summarizes this well. *"Many people assume that storytelling is somehow in conflict with authenticity. The great storyteller, in this view, is a spinner of yarns that amuse without being rooted in truth.... But great storytelling does not conflict with truth. In the business world and elsewhere, it is always built on the integrity of the story and its teller."*[43]

If you make up stories, you are just kicking the can down the road, doing the exact opposite of what we are talking about here in building assets. You are conflicting directly with the values of the content marketer of empathy, honesty, transparency, and generosity. It isn't the way to go.

I really wanted to avoid the situation where you make it this far and find there is no story. I'm hopeful you have read through those options and found more than a few great stories in your business or your customers or your products that you can work with.

But if you didn't, there's still hope. Sometimes, you don't naturally find yourself in a story; you need to force yourself into one. Seth Godin puts it this way: "Find and build and earn your story, the arc of the change you seek to produce."[44] In other words, just because you don't automatically find yourself in the middle of a great story, it doesn't mean you can't seek one out.

Start deliberately looking for the type of work that will lead to great stories. Think about our Piña Colada beer. That post had over a

---

43   https://hbr.org/2007/12/the-four-truths-of-the-storyteller
44   https://www.amazon.com.au/This-Marketing-Seth-Godin/dp/0525540830

hundred comments, and that's just a small fraction of the number of beer ideas we hear every day. But choosing to brew that beer placed us in the middle of a really fun customer hero story. We had 100% control over that. We didn't have to make that beer; we chose to, and that choice placed us in a story.

Maybe there are choices you can make in your business that will place you in a story or put you on the trajectory to form a great story.

If not, let me say this. I don't want to be one of those experts who tells you that their model fits perfectly with what you are doing, regardless of what you are doing. Perhaps it doesn't.

If you can't see any option, your choice is to either fake a story or ignore storytelling (at least for now). I say if it's not a good fit, embrace the other strategies and come back to this one another time. If at some point in the future you find yourself in a story, at least now you will recognize it.

3

COMMUNITY

In 2012, I set myself an enormous task to build a software startup with a twelve-month runway without any skills as a developer and no path to startup investment. I had never done it before, and I had to learn a lot very quickly. The first thing I needed to learn was how I could get people to sign up to pay for the product. I had fallen in love with design, and I wanted it to be nice and elegant.

I first looked at PayPal. PayPal buttons offered subscriptions and were stupidly easy to implement. This would have taken me five minutes, but it wasn't elegant, and I wanted something inbuilt and clean and professional.

I spent three weeks implementing Google Wallet. Once I made it live, I realized that you couldn't take payment in Australia at the time; it was for United States residents only. Big mistake, back to square one.

There was very little information out there about what options I had. Google produced average results, and the main drivers behind these decisions were your local bank. But if you've ever dealt with banks in Australia, you'll understand why I wanted no part of that.

Eventually, I decided to integrate with a bit of a compromise solution, Braintree. They worked with your traditional banks and offered a nice, clean integration. I worked for months on setting up Braintree. I had phone calls with reps and meetings with the bank and non-stop communication with my developer until we got it done. In the end, we had a decent solution, but the fees were through the roof, and the work required was ridiculous.

Ultimately, the choice of payment gateway didn't matter because the business was shut down after ten months with only ten customers who I'm sure didn't care at all which payment gateway I used.

This story was very normal at the time. Lots of developers were sniffing around looking for nice, clean, simple ways to build credit card payments into websites, but there was nothing obvious that existed and appealed strongly to these developers.

At the time, a startup was emerging, not in Australia but in the U.S. They called themselves Stripe. Their story started many years before. In 2007, online payments were solved by an extremely progressive startup merger between two companies started by Peter Thiel and Elon Musk called PayPal.

But like I found in 2012, while PayPal offered a unique and simple solution, it wasn't as elegant as what the modern web developer desired. Between 2007 and 2012, not much had changed in terms of payment processing. It was PayPal or bank-endorsed clunky payment gateways.

Patrick and John Collison founded Stripe to solve this exact problem.[45] They gained access to the famed Silicon Valley startup incubator Y Combinator in 2010 and grew in leaps and bounds since. At the time of writing in 2020, Stripe is considered Silicon Valley's most valuable startup, coming in at $36b in enterprise value based on its most recent round.[46]

When Stripe set out to help developers find an easy solution to taking payments online, they didn't just build the solution. They invested in other things as well. From the very early days, Stripe was known as the payment solution that developers loved.

---

[45] https://www.wired.co.uk/article/stripe-payments-apple-amazon-facebook

[46] https://www.cnbc.com/2020/04/16/stripe-raises-600-million-funding-roun d-at-36-billion-valuation.html#:~:text=Stripe%20has%20raised%20even%20 more,first%20reported%20Stripe's%20new%20valuation.

Some of this was because of the design. Their design was simple and elegant and beautiful. Everything they did from day one looked perfect. Of course, they had a great story and a great product, but their engagement with their community was where they really stood out.

Much like me when I looked for a payment solution for my app, most developers hated payment providers. They were ugly, clunky, old-school, and expensive. Stripe became the payment provider that developers loved, and it wasn't by accident.

Stripe had a close connection with their customers. They started the business because they, as developers, had their own frustrations with taking payments online. Their first customer became their first employees.[47]

They built their entire product and content strategy around serving developers.[48]

They grew initially via word of mouth, especially via the network in Y Combinator, helped along by a single blog post by one of the Y Combinator partners, Gary Tan. It was a super short post. It said there was a YC company working on payment processing, and it was "developer-focused, which is a dramatic departure from the status quo in the payments business."[49] Stripe signups exploded.

And it was true. Stripe really cared about their community of developers.

Early implementers were sent physical care packages of shirts and stickers. Stripe held meetups, sponsored hackathons,[50] and organized competitions for developers like their Capture The Flag initiative.[51] This was a wargame-inspired competition where developers identified and exploited security problems. Tens of thousands of developers competed!

---

[47] https://www.startupgrind.com/blog/the-collison-brothers-and-story-behind-the-founding-of-stripe/

[48] https://openviewpartners.com/blog/how-stripe-built-a-sales-organization-to-successfully-sell-to-developers/#.Xuija2ozYWo

[49] https://blog.ycombinator.com/need-to-process-payments/

[50] https://growthhackers.com/growth-studies/how-stripe-marketed-to-developers-so-effectively

[51] https://stripe.com/blog/capture-the-flag

Stripe developed an amazing resource of technical documentation. Remember when I said I couldn't find any info online about how to set up a decent payment processor? Stripe solved this, very shortly after I wasted all that time and money.

Stripe had a beautifully executed documentation structure with anything you would need to know to get going with Stripe. Of course, they also have an awesome blog filled with seriously detailed guides on many aspects of running the types of businesses that may at one point use an online payment processor. They had an industry update section with the latest on what's happening in processing and the typical blog with product updates, product-specific resources, and lots of options for getting further support. And the blog looked sexy!

It still does look sexy. When you visit the Stripe homepage now, they only have four menu items on their website. One of them is "Developers."[52]

This is a company that has defined its community and done everything in their power to keep that community happy. And it's paid off to the tune of $36b. Sexy branding, great engagement of a community, awesome content, and a neat story—Compound Marketing gold.

ENGAGING A COMMUNITY

Engaging a community can be hard, especially if there are already a lot of competitors attempting to do that. This is your job as a business owner or product marketer: figure out how to capture the attention of a community of people.

Community building is something that my co-founders and I have built into Black Hops Brewery from the beginning. Not as a marketing tactic, but because we were part of the craft beer community and wanted to add value to it. It's an easy and natural thing in beer. I've also done it with other businesses, and while it hasn't been as easy, it's certainly been worth it.

Here are some ideas of how on go about it.

---

[52]   https://stripe.com/au/guides

PEEL BACK THE CURTAIN

A great way to build trust in a small group is to offer them a new level of transparency. I did this with my income reports back when I was trying to start my analytics app. It wasn't super comfortable publishing my income (or lack of it) to the world, but my audience really appreciated it. It was rare to get real information on projects like this, so it was useful for them to see behind the curtain into what was really going on inside a speculative startup.

When we started Black Hops, I was really excited to try this because I hadn't seen that level of transparency in an industry like beer manufacturing before. And when we started planning the brewery, it was clear that no one else was very transparent about how to do it; there was almost nothing useful to be found on the topic.

We shared everything early on, from our finances to our recipes to the exact suppliers we were using for our equipment, and much more. We published all of this on our blog and on our podcast and book (both called Operation Brewery). On the podcast, I even recorded a phone call with one of our first investors, where I was trying to negotiate his investment. We published it as an episode!

This proved super effective for us. While nothing got a huge amount of individual traction, a small core group of people loved it, and those people became the Black Hops Ambassadors, the core group who fueled much of our growth for years to come.

We continue in this tradition to this day, releasing all of our costs behind the beer we make just a few weeks back.[53] It's what we do, and it's useful to people in our community, and it also happens to be a great generator of free attention.

HAVE A MEETING PLACE

If you plan on putting a lot of effort into building a super-engaged community, then think about where you will meet.

---

[53]   https://blackhops.com.au/craft-beer-prices-how-much-does-beer-cost-to-make-2-0/

In-person

One thing that's been consistent across many of the great examples of modern companies that I can think of in terms of engaging a community is their deliberate strategy for getting people together in person.

At the brewery, there is, of course, one super obvious choice, and that's at the bar at one of our breweries. And we utilize that a huge amount when it comes to making extra effort to engage with our most eager community members.

At the time of writing, during the middle of COVID-19, there's a non-stop focus on remote work and online communication. The message seems to be that in-person no longer matters, and working and socializing remotely will solve all problems. Call me old school, but I'm not buying it. Nothing beats in-person as a powerful way to grow the value of a community and a brand.

Modern companies are embracing in-person events, not to sell more products, but to champion their most powerful customers and engage their highest potential customers.

Xero is a great example of this. Xero is a $12b company that has revolutionized accounting. Companies like this are normally started in Silicon Valley, not Xero. It was started in an apartment in New Zealand, and it aimed at taking on the behemoths of the financial world MYOB and QuickBooks.[54] The Kiwis love a good underdog story!

The year 2006 was the same year I left Queensland Rail to start my website building business, and in Australia, at the time, MYOB was the *only* accounting solution that was used. I hated it with an absolute passion. It was awful software, but I was forced to use it for three years because there was no reasonable alternative. I paid my accountants thousands of dollars each year to do most of my accounting when I felt I should be able to do it myself. But that was the way. In terms of customer experience, MYOB was like getting a taxi before they launched Uber.

---

[54] https://en.wikipedia.org/wiki/Xero_(software)#:~:text=Xero%20was%20 founded%20in%20a,are%20still%20located%20in%20Wellington.

In 2006, MYOB turned over $182 million dollars, up 13% from the year before, and was solidly profitable.[55] It was a great business, and Xero was literally starting from, well, zero. I could see MYOB was a terrible solution with all this double entry and a stupid large file that sat on your computer, and if it got damaged, you'd lose everything, while Xero was in the cloud, easy to use, and dare I say it, satisfying.

The problem was that this was an industry dominated by old accountants and getting traction in this crowd was going to be near impossible. There was no interest in anything new.

Xero played the long game. They focused on great design and a great product, and they engaged the startup entrepreneurs and the up-and-coming accountants who were open to change. People who'd been doing accounting for twenty years saw Xero as a threat. People who were just starting saw this new cloud approach as a great opportunity.

Xero engaged this new breed of accountants in many ways, but one in particular was especially powerful: in person via their XeroCon event. They've been running the event for eight years and now run it in multiple cities around the world. They get thousands of attendees, and as someone who shares an office with an accountant, I can tell you that attendees are very much into going to this event.

Xero champions their most powerful partners and customers, and they make people feel like they are part of something special. *"If you could sum up Xerocon in three words, what would it be? Fun, inspirational, community."*[56]

Last year, they held the event in Brisbane (my home city), San Diego, and London.[57] Looking at the photos from the event, you'd be forgiven for thinking it was some kind of cult, not a meetup for one of the most traditional and undisruptable fields you could imagine.

In-person is a powerful community builder, and regardless of the progress of technology or other circumstances, always will be.

---

[55] http://www.annualreports.com/HostedData/AnnualReports/PDF/Annual_Report2006.pdf

[56] https://www.xero.com/blog/2019/07/xerocons-most-loyal-attendees/

[57] https://www.xero.com/sg/events/xerocon/brisbane-2019/

Online

The power of in-person aside, online can always be powerful, and this is where a huge amount of community building happens. The tools available these days are mind-blowing, and with so much attention online, the opportunities can't be ignored.

With social media commanding so much of a company's marketing effort, it's the obvious place. Ever since I released my first book, *The 7 Day Startup*, I've found Facebook groups to be the most effective place to build great communities. This may change. I get a little nervous recommending a specific social media platform for something like this, especially Facebook! That said, Facebook Groups have been great to me.

My first Facebook Group for *The 7 Day Startup* was where I did all the community building for the book launch, and it resulted in the book becoming a best-seller and launching me into a very unexpected side career as a book writer.

The Black Hops Ambassador group has followed in those footsteps and has become an epic place for our most valuable community members to hang out. It's also the main port of call when we need help ourselves when there are things like online votes that require the support of an active community.

You need a place if you want to form a community, and online is the most obvious option. A few words of warning about the places you choose:

- Be careful about choosing someone else's platform. As my mate James Schramko says, aim to *"Own the racecourse, not the racehorse."*[58] I have often thought about this advice, and while I ignore it by choosing Facebook to host our Black Hops Ambassador group, I do it first by considering all the pros and cons. It is a very big factor to consider. You may decide the trade-off is worth it but know full well that your

---

[58] https://www.superfastbusiness.com/business/546-otr-own-the-racecourse-2017-the-most-powerful-marketing-strategy-ever/

active Facebook Group could and probably will become a place that's impossible to market to without paying Facebook for the privilege.

- I would be very hesitant to choose outdated communication methods; the example that comes to mind is an online forum. I still see people making this mistake. People don't have time for the inefficiency of forums, especially on mobile devices. If you have a great one already, then that's cool; if not, look elsewhere.

- Social media is the most obvious choice to build a community but weigh the pros and cons of some of the downsides of social media. Everyone has access to your public page, the tide can turn at any moment against your favor, and you own none of the infrastructure. Again, I wouldn't write it off as a bad choice. It may be the best choice but think about the downside risk.

- With online communities, things can go south quickly. Make sure you keep your community a safe place and try your best to keep out negativity. I sometimes go to extremes to keep out negativity, but if you've cultivated your own space, you need to be careful it doesn't get out of hand. Cultures are complex, and negativity can act like cancer and eat it from the inside out. I've deleted people's posts, direct-messaged them telling them how unhappy I am with them, in some cases replied pretty aggressively on negative posts, and the list goes on. Some people probably think I'm a bit of an arsehole when it comes to that stuff, but the strict "no negativity" rule has served me well. If someone wants to be a hater, there are lots of public places they can do that. The idea of a tight-knit community is that it's a positive, supportive place.

Online communities have been hugely powerful for my businesses and continue to be. Aim to give more value than you get and keep them positive.

DON'T LET EVERYONE IN, KEEP THEM SMALL

I mentioned my initial 7 Day Startup group above. I loved this group; it was the whole reason why the book launched with great success. That book was supposed to be given away for free, but a mate of mine, Tom Morkes, helped me with publishing and advised me that I really had to charge for it to get any traction on Amazon. I wanted to give it away for free, but I took his advice and put it on Amazon for a few dollars. Before we did that, we offered it to a core group of advocates via the free 7 Day Startup Facebook group. These advocates got behind it, and it launched as a best seller on Amazon, sold tens of thousands of copies, and ended up being translated into over 10 languages. There were about 200 people in the group in those days.

As the years went on, the group grew and grew, and I fell in love with these vanity metrics. When it passed 10,000, I posted a little celebration.

When it got to 14,000, I shut the group down. It no longer exists. It became a spam-fest and more like a pretty average public social media account. Plus, it was a full-time job to maintain. To its members and to me, it was infinitely more valuable when it had 200 members than it was with 14,000.

The idea of a core community is that it's not for everyone. It's for the biggest super fans, and if it was for everyone, then it would feel less exclusive to the main members. It can't be for everyone. Smaller is better.

There has to be some nuance here because making something "exclusive" can have the opposite effect of what we're trying to achieve. It can kill trust and rub people the wrong way. Making an elite community isn't the point; it's keeping in the most engaged people and serving them as well as you can. Finding that balance is a challenge worthy of pursuit.

RUN COMPETITIONS

Running competitions is a bit of an age-old technique for building a community, but damn, it works. I normally don't love doing social media competitions; I think it draws people who just want free shit and who probably don't care much about your brand at all. And it focuses on vanity metrics of follower numbers and not the stuff that's really important.

But competitions within a small, dedicated group can be supremely powerful. I mentioned the Stripe "Capture The Flag" competition above. Tens of thousands of people competed, and guess what the prize was? A t-shirt!

The X Prize, a famed competition where super ambitious people and companies compete for bragging rights, was founded on the same idea. Absurdly expensive endeavors are encouraged by minimal prizes, and the results are staggering. The first X Prize, where they challenged entrants to achieve sub-orbital space flights, ended up leading to the likes of Jeff Bezos and Richard Branson launching multi-billion dollar efforts to send tourists into space. The prize was a measly $10m.[59]

The magic here is the engaged group of participants competing for a rare accolade. The size of the purse isn't relevant; Bezos doesn't get out of bed for $10m.

At Black Hops, during the COVID-19 crisis in March 2020, we decided to double down on our own competition. Launched inside our Black Hops Ambassador group, we released the "Black Hops Reserves" competition. We put out our recipes, showing all participants behind the curtain, but we did more than that.

We released brew-at-home kits that made it super easy for people to brew Black Hops beers at home. These Black Hops Reserves kits would sell out within minutes of launching. We launched a competition open to anyone brewing their own kit or non-kit version of our beer to become the ultimate Black Hops Reserve Champion Brewer. We would release the recipes of every one of our seven core range beers, along with the brew-at-home kits, and we would run a monthly tasting of entries judged by the other Black Hops team members and me.

---

[59] https://en.wikipedia.org/wiki/X_Prize_Foundation#1996%E2%80%932004_
Ansari_XPRIZE_for_Suborbital_Spaceflight

The first recipe had 75 entries, and it didn't slow down. We limited the kits to around 100 each time and consistently got 50+ entries. The winners got a little pin they could proudly wear, showing that they had achieved a gold medal for that beer. The overall winners got a coin for the beer, and the overall winner across all seven beers got the overall Black Hops Reserves Champion Brewer coin.

This was not a competition designed to go viral. It was a competition to reward and grow our closest community members. We didn't make money off it, and it wasn't free. The amount our community valued our brand as a result of doing it wasn't, and never could be, measured. It was Compound Marketing gold.

GIVE THEM SOMETHING EXCLUSIVE

Being part of a community has to come with some upside. It's a two-way street. Your most engaged community members should provide you with a lot of support and value, but they need to be rewarded in return. In fact, the best way to keep a community super-engaged is to weigh it massively in their favor. Make the rare ask for support, but for the most part, offer them great value. Remember, this isn't a group to make money on; that's not the point. This is a place to engage a super-committed group, so give them something unique.

At Black Hops, we give our most loyal followers lots of exclusive benefits like a membership program, the ability to reserve beers, early access to online beers and events, exclusive pre-launch tastings, and more. We rarely even mention our Reserves program outside the Ambassador group; it all happens inside the group. We have one-off merch that never gets reprinted that only the biggest supporters grab. We have hundreds of individual beer labels that have been collected by our community members over the years, and most will never be reprinted.

These are a few examples of things that give our closest community members the ability to have something unique and exclusive, something special. It makes them feel special because they are; they are our most loyal and dedicated supporters.

THINK OF THEM WHEN YOU CREATE CONTENT

If you are going to commit to this audience-building strategy, your most engaged community members are a great place to start with to come up with content ideas. When we create content, we think of these most-engaged group members and think about what they would want to hear about. We ask them directly as well, which can often lead to some fun content ideas.

If it's great content for your most engaged community members, it's probably great content generally. But even if it's not, your key community will love it, and that's a decent start. Any content that the key group loves will only raise your status in their eyes. And like all content marketing, sometimes the best part is the fact that it's fun to do and can benefit other people. It's the most rewarding way to market a business!

Having a core group gives you a goldmine for content ideas, so pay attention to what they are after and think of the core group when you work on content.

BEND RULES FOR COMMUNITY MEMBERS

Occasionally, we might slightly bend the rules for our most-engaged community members. While I do try to stay away from an elitist approach to marketing, the odd rule twist is sometimes an appropriate way to make people feel special.

A quick heads-up about something that's coming up or tweaking of quantities to let a few extra people in on a release—those things can go a long way. These are the sorts of touchy decisions that are hard work to make happen, and for that reason, most companies ignore them and rely on hard and fast rules.

Bending the rules slightly for your most-engaged community members can create an opportunity. People aren't often made to feel special. The occasional twisting of the rules can go a long way to engage your most loyal community members, and one small favor can hold the brand in good stead for a long time.

What's even better is that if you are doing this because you legitimately value these people, and it's genuine, then it shows. People recognize real.

PROMOTE COMMUNITY MEMBERS

There's nothing better in a community than a successful community member. Remember, everyone wants a hero, and what's better for a community than a community hero? Don't be afraid to shout out key members, reward them, and promote them.

Competition winners or super-value-adding members or specific high-value new members are worthy of promotion.

When we promoted our Ambassador member Marc for coming up with the idea for our Piña Colada beer, it was great fun for everyone in the community and a well-deserved reward for Marc. We've made merch designed by group members before, we've promoted the winners of our brew competition in the group, and we've shared their photos on our social media accounts.

There are loads of ways you can promote members of your group once you see it as good and useful.

BE ACCESSIBLE

I'm often torn about how accessible I make myself. I think that sometimes you can elevate yourself personally by making yourself less accessible, and you can certainly reduce your stress levels and your workload by doing so. But there is no denying the power of being accessible to your keenest community members.

People need to attach to brands. Remember, brands are how people feel about a company or a product, so to create legitimate feelings requires something deep. Making yourself accessible can do this.

For Black Hops, all three founders are regulars at our taprooms, at events, as writers on our blog, as guests or hosts on the podcast, and in the Facebook group. I can tell you that there's nothing our group members love more than when Govs goes into the group and drops value bombs about brewing or answers questions from members.

Eddie doesn't reply in there as often, he's more of a lurker, but his presence is felt when he does post, and it's clearly appreciated. I'm in there way too often, and I think it's very much appreciated. There aren't too many companies that have grown to where we are and are growing at our pace, where the founders are that accessible. I think this creates an enormous amount of goodwill.

There are some risks and downsides to being this available, but for a new business, especially, it's a very worthwhile strategy. As you grow, perhaps it can be dialed in a bit as you elevate staff members into that role.

GIVE THEM AN IDENTITY

The idea of giving your community an identity or a name is something I've left to last because I do see this as optional. It can be super-powerful if done right, but it's also very overused, and if you can't pull it off in a unique way, it could do more harm than good.

Our Black Hops core community is called the Black Hops Ambassadors. We could have gone with the Black Hops Army, but out of respect to people who've served, we avoided that despite "Army" being a common word to use for your core group.

Lady Gaga calls her most loyal fans her Little Monsters,[60] Fans of Twilight were called Twihards,[61] and Justin Bieber fans are called Beliebers.[62]

And yes, in case you wondered, I know this because I'm all three.

Many companies have done this with great effect, and if you can find a name that's not massively overused and can mean something to members, it can make people feel like they're part of something special.

It can also open up other options like doing specific merch for members, etc. (give them something exclusive). At Black Hops, we have a specific shirt for Black Hops Reserves homebrew members

[60] https://ladygaga.fandom.com/wiki/Little_Monsters_(fanbase)

[61] https://ew.com/celebrity/best-celebrity-fandom-names/?slide=6179366#6179366

[62] https://www.beautyheaven.com.au/detox/Celebrity-fan-group-names/justin-bieber

that they can only buy if they have entered the Reserves comp. You can have a lot of fun with this idea, but be wary of overusing it and the potential for it to become less genuine.

MULTIPLE COMMUNITIES

Businesses don't just have one community they serve. It's easy to think about your main customer base and only focus on them when it comes to making content, building out the brand, serving the community, and so on. This is a mistake. Most businesses have multiple communities, and forgetting key groups can severely limit your impact.

In our business of selling beer, we obviously have the local beer drinker as our main community. But digging deeper, we have lots of other communities:

- Home Brewers (Black Hops Reserves) - These people are buyers of our homebrew products, they are an awesome community that spreads the word, and they are also customers of our normal beers and promoters in venues and influencers within their circles. A great community to serve!

- Wholesale customer - We have bars and restaurants and bottle shops that sell our beer, whose staff are also a passionate group of supporters. These are ultimately the people who influence the end customer, so you can't get much more important than that.

- Local drinkers - Of course, we have our local taproom customers who have their own identity and are huge supporters and promoters of what we do. They are the lifeblood of our brand and the first people we think of when we start talking about a new beer.

- Online customers - We have online customers around the country that buy our beer, share it on social media, and help us raise the profile of the brand.

- Investors - We have 550+ investors who finance the business but are also super passionate advocates for our brand. These guys are regularly in venues and among friends promoting our brand, so they are a hugely important audience to keep engaged.

- General interest - We have a group of people who are just generally interested in beer and are keen consumers of our content and supporters on social media, etc. A lot of the content we create is general interest content that doesn't directly serve one of the other groups.

We have different content and brand-building and community-building strategies for all of these groups. We have specific merch for Black Hops Reserves that others can't buy. We have an online group for investors and supporters, we have perks only available to locals, and we have programs to engage wholesale customers. These communities will perceive the brand differently from other groups and will have different needs when it comes to engagement and content.

Take the time to write down all the communities you serve and what activities you can engage in that can help build those communities. What can elevate the brand in their eyes? What content do they like? What stories will they relate to?

Then down the track, you can use these groups in your content to better target the topics to members of each community.

Community is an absolutely essential part of the Compound Marketing strategy. At the heart of organic, word-of-mouth growth is people. Keeping a tight group of your most vocal and powerful people is what community-building is all about.

4

CONTENT

Ultimately, to build a business using Compound Marketing strategies, it all comes down to content. There has to be a way for your community to engage with your brand, and while content might have many names these days, it's all content.

Content marketing has been my favorite marketing strategy since I wrote my first blog post in 2009. The idea that you can do something that is (a) fun to do, (b) creates value for other people, and that thing be something that's (c) considered to be marketing! Well, that's just plain exciting. And it wasn't particularly new. It was just that, the way technology had progressed, it became a feasible way to market a business.

WHAT IS CONTENT MARKETING

I wrote a whole book about content marketing in 2015 called *Content Machine*, so it feels a little strange to only be dedicating one section in this book to it. But it also feels more timely than ever.

In 2015, my definition of content marketing was:

> *"Content marketing is releasing something interesting that grabs attention for a business and builds trust."*

We don't really talk about content marketing anymore; content has become so prolific and ingrained that it's just what people do.

Whatever you want to call it, the most prolific modern marketers are releasing something interesting that grabs people's attention and builds trust.

When I first started with content marketing, different disciplines of content marketing were broken up via clear and dividing lines. If you wrote content, you were a blogger. If you spoke content, you were a podcaster. If you were a social media expert, you probably just weren't a good writer or talker.

These days, it's all just content.

Yes, I listen to the Joe Rogan podcast from time to time, but I consume Joe Rogan content constantly. I see his videos on Instagram, I see his posts on Facebook, I hear other people talking about him and his guests on their podcasts, I see the discussions around episodes on Facebook, I see him on Netflix, I see him on TV when I watch UFC, and I see guests share his content on Twitter. Because I'm into Joe Rogan, I see Joe Rogan content everywhere. I don't think it would make sense to describe Joe Rogan as a podcaster.

Bloggers are the same. I used to read the Basecamp blog, Signal vs. Noise. Now, I watch episodes of the founder DHH on podcasts, I see the constant stream of his tweets, I see his nice cars on Instagram, I read the books he puts out, etc. I feel like I see more of him now than ever, but I rarely read the blog anymore.

These definitions no longer make sense. Marketers who have the Compound Marketing mindset just go ahead and do their thing, and we consume it in whatever way is convenient. Joe Rogan and DHH have been doing the same thing the whole time, putting their ideas out into the world and using that to grow their businesses. And those various things have compounded for them and made them very successful.

In the era of Instagram and TikTok influencers, content marketing has exploded. All of our attention now is on these social media platforms, and the smart people who command that attention have turned that into extremely valuable marketing for their businesses.

HOW BUSINESSES SHOULD THINK ABOUT CONTENT MARKETING

For a long time, it was hard to convince people that spending time creating content could be a good decision. Those days are gone. With the staggering growth in platforms that encourage users to produce content and the results that come to those who do well on those platforms, it's hard to argue these days that content isn't critical.

But you still need to have a certain way of thinking to do well as a content marketer. You can't just click a button to implement content marketing like you would to sponsor a Facebook post. It takes a different way of thinking about how you spend your time and marketing energy.

The best content marketers think differently.

EMBRACE TRANSPARENCY

Transparency used to be a dirty word. Old-school mentors would encourage you to "keep your cards close to your chest" and not "air your dirty laundry." Guess what? People love dirty laundry. Every great story has success and failure, and whether it's up or down, as long as it's real, it's interesting.

In some parts of life, transparency has gone to extremes. Social media influencers are sharing every second of every day, and to be honest, it's pretty damn effective. We laughed at social media influencers until we realized the ones doing it well were fast becoming millionaires and billionaires.[63]

We can't laugh anymore because it turns out that they are engaging consumers far better than we are. And they're doing it by sharing a lot of information and producing an extraordinary amount of content, sometimes hundreds of micro-posts a day. In years gone by, content marketing consisted of spending three weeks on a large blog post.

---

[63] https://www.forbes.com/sites/natalierobehmed/2019/03/05/at-21-kylie-jenner-becomes-the-youngest-self-made-billionaire-ever/

Not to say that's not useful too, but let's admit that there's merit to the new approach.

If you can be comfortable revealing more than others, your content will be more interesting.

CREATION WITHOUT EXPECTATION OF IMMEDIATE REWARD

There are people who like meeting and discussing things, and there are people who like creating things. Creating things is hard, but it's what successful people do.

Companies who want to embrace content marketing need to hire more creators and need to be comfortable with creating a lot of content, whether it's blog posts, social media posts, videos, or products that engage the audience or press stories—the list goes on. Whatever it is, it needs to be perfectly normal inside your business to create things with little to no expectation of an immediate reward.

Seth Godin, the godfather of modern marketing, recently put it this way, *"If you are competing against 6.5 billion people, it's naive and arrogant to think you're entitled to a quick hit."*[64]

Content marketing is rarely an overnight success. Sure, there are exceptions, but even a lot of the people who have done well on social media who are apparently "overnight successes" have put out thousands or tens of thousands of posts and micro-posts. Which, if you think about it, is loads more than a normal company would have historically done. So maybe they are just creating more?

Either way, if the company and the people within the company don't allow the free creation of content without expectation, then it's not going to work.

It's also extremely hard to predict which content is going to go well. In 2020, when one of my posts does well, I get a kick out of it because I still have no idea what will work.

In the early days, I used to delve hard into analytics to try to figure out how to quantify it. But in the end, I had a couple of pieces of

---

[64]   https://productiveinsights.com/seth-godin-on-marketing/

content that did well, and they rendered all other content basically meaningless. And even after more than a decade of doing it, I feel none the wiser about which content will do it. And on top of that, if it does end up being successful, quite often it won't be successful straight away. Some of the best posts build over time.

Many years of this results in an attitude of: I will create content freely and do my best to serve the community and uphold the brand, but I have zero clue whether it will go well. And this, to me, is a great way to approach content marketing. Be generous and don't see it as a quick fix. See it as a way to provide value now and take the leap of faith to believe it will pay you back down the track.

ALWAYS GIVE VALUE

My old mentors used to tell me to raise my prices and never give something away for free if you could charge for it. They would say it was devaluing your offering. Companies that value content marketing call bullshit on this idea. They are happy to give out enormous amounts of value without the expectation of being paid for it.

They do it with confidence, not because they don't value what they sell, but because they value what they sell so highly that they know they can be generous at the front end, and the back-end sales will take care of themselves.

It's a fundamentally different way to view things, but if you think about it, this is what most of the recently successful startups do. Software businesses give you extremely useful tools for free to get you using the system. Smart companies are running conferences and charging cost-price or less. The best startups are investing in their content and engaging their community because they see it as exactly that—an investment.

Value is the epicenter of content marketing. Content marketing was never about writing blog posts or producing podcasts; it was always about creating something that someone else wants.

A generous effort to provide value to people in your community is likely to bring long-term rewards.

FORGET ROI

Marketers have been obsessed forever with the idea of figuring out the ROI on marketing spend. It's referred to as the age-old marketing problem.[65]

I was obsessed with this myself for a while. When I was working on my analytics app, I actually released a version that was aimed at figuring out the ROI on content marketing. It didn't work, and as far as I'm concerned, it's not something that can be done.

The value of a brand and how people feel about your product is nearly impossible to measure in the short-term. If the goal of Compound Marketing is to grow the value of your brand over time, the only way you will measure it will be after years and years. And even then, how do you know what pieces of content got certain people's trust to create a tipping point for your growth?

Companies that want to embrace content marketing need to get out of the ROI mindset and be confident that creating great content for a key group of people is going to pay off in the long-term. Embrace the long game.

ARE YOU NOT ENTERTAINED?

One way of doing content marketing well is to create as much value as possible. Another way that is increasing in relevance is the ability to entertain.

It used to be that you would get your entertainment from going to the movies and watching TV. Not now.

TV, or the new version of it, streaming, is still a great source of entertainment. But an even bigger source is democratized content channels like YouTube, Podcasts, Facebook, Instagram, Twitter, and TikTok.

A few months ago, Sarah Cooper was inspired by seeing President Donald Trump's daily coronavirus task force meetings and realizing that he was, in her words, *"kind of BSing his way through the presidency."*

---

[65]   https://www.socialmediaexaminer.com/research-social-marketers-roi/

She was also trying to build a following on the rising content platform TikTok, and after failing with dance videos, decided to give lip-syncing audio clips a go. It was another popular way to create content on the platform.

She started lip-syncing Trump's press briefings on TikTok and Twitter, and her clips went consistently viral.[66] She blew past 2m followers, and at the time of writing this, is growing at about a hundred thousand per week with 22m views for her first video.

Her videos have been shared by major influencers like Jerry Seinfeld, Ellen DeGeneres, and Ben Stiller, along with politicians, journalists, and millions of others.[67]

She's on her way to using this attention to build a business to capitalize on the attention. This is what content marketing looks like now.

Sarah is a comedian, so it makes sense for her to be entertaining, but I seek this same thing in a lot of my content. For my startup dose, I listen to *This Week in Startups* and podcasts like *Pivot*. The hosts of those programs, Jason Calacanis (*This Week In Startups*) and Scott Galloway (*Pivot*), know a lot about startups, but I don't think that's really why I listen to them. Sitting through an hour or two of someone just rolling out startup news or facts sounds horribly boring. I like these podcasts because they are entertaining.

Jason is fun to listen to, can be a bit brash, and some might say he's obnoxious. He has very strong opinions, and he's pretty fearless, which I find fun to listen to. Scott is an esteemed business professor, successful startup entrepreneur, serial board member, and best-selling author. But I like him because he's funny. There are lots of business professors, and I'm sure lots of them have podcasts, but I don't listen to any of them other than Scott's.

To make it even more fun, both of these guys dislike each other and are currently fighting on Twitter. I get to learn about startups and business and get entertained at the same time; it's a win-win!

---

[66] https://www.huffingtonpost.com.au/entry/
tiktok-comedian-sarah-cooper-jimmy-fallon_au_5ee6ab74c5b61688c6213210

[67] https://trungtphan.com/sarah-cooper-10000-hours/

Making people laugh or entertaining people in some way is extremely powerful. It's not easy to convert that into sales, but it's an extremely good way of getting traction. When I first got into podcasts, it was all business podcasts, and I was looking for as many practical business tips as possible. If I look at my podcast subscription list now, it's not about that at all. I listen to podcasts that are interesting and entertaining. The idea of listening to one person dropping tips is unthinkable.

The same can be said about all content mediums because they are competing directly with the most entertaining content in the world. Now, on your device of choice, you have Netflix and Disney Plus and Amazon Prime TV and Apple TV Plus, not to mention TikTok and Spotify and podcasts and Facebook and Instagram and YouTube. To get me interested in anything that's not entertaining is going to be extremely hard work.

Now is the time to invest in bringing more entertainment into your content. If you write blog posts, that's fine. Blog posts don't have to be boring. Mark Manson's blog posts are very bloody entertaining, and they always have been, perhaps that's a big part of why he's been so successful?[68]

If you are doing podcasts by yourself, change it up. Find a co-host and find a way to make it more fun.

Entertainment isn't just the job of entertainers anymore.

LOVE YOUR COMMUNITY

Companies that are nailing content marketing in 2020 have a deep love and connection with their audience. What often works is having people in the company who were once (or still are) part of this audience.

This is very much the case at Black Hops. All the founders are part of the homebrew and craft beer scene and are in the game because they fell in love with this community. Our staff is the same. We know and understand and love the community we create things for, and that makes all the difference.

---

[68] https://markmanson.net/best-articles

I've noticed this by following other entrepreneurs who have branched out of the online marketing world into success in other fields, and the trend is the same.

Nathan Barry is a great example. When I was into online marketing a decade ago, Nathan was considered an online marketing influencer. His blog posts about how to sell more ebooks were well known, and he was one of the respected online marketing people. Back then, there were many online marketers, and these days as I look back, very few of them have transcended that space into legitimate high-growth, long-term business success. I can probably count on one hand out of the hundreds or thousands of them who are not either out of the game or still scrapping for the next digital product launch.

Nathan launched an email marketing SAAS application called ConvertKit. I've launched many startups and plenty of software startups, and they are near impossible to do. Nathan picked arguably the most impossible business idea of all, email marketing software. This space is so ludicrously competitive, and just the basic tech is so challenging that not many sensible people would ever try to do this. Not only that, but he got into it without the typical VC funding, which is unheard of in a field like this.

He also did it very publicly doing income reports and embracing the new world transparency we've seen from some of the best startups. *"One of our values at ConvertKit is to work in public. We strive for transparency, which is why we share information that is typically kept private, such as our finances."*[69]

It's been a tremendous success. Looking at their public dashboard, I can see that, after a few short years, their annualized revenue is over $20m.[70] That makes them more successful than any of that original crew of online marketers and puts Nathan in a whole new category of entrepreneur: self-funded, eight-figure, SAAS founder.

Nathan did a lot of things right, but I think the big thing was his love for the community, which clearly continues to this day. ConvertKit has a core group of much-loved customers. The word

---

[69] https://convertkit.com/april-2020-deliverability-report

[70] https://convertkit.baremetrics.com/

they use is "Creators," and their whole content platform revolves around delivering value to this group.

Their public finances, their championing of customers, their high-value content on their blog, their podcast—the list goes on. And it comes from a genuine place of love for this audience. Nathan is a creator himself and loves this group of people who use his software.

This genuine approach is how to do content marketing well. Love your audience, and create as much value for them as you can.

HAVE A PURPOSE

All of this content creation sounds fun, but it's a huge trap to just create lots of content with no purpose. The best content is created for a reason, and it's well thought out. The reason might be super simple, or it might seem shallow—to entertain, to inform, etc.—but there has to be a reason you create content, and it has to make sense.

In my book *Content Machine*, I introduced an important missing piece of many types of content marketing I was seeing. I called it "monetization logic," and it referred to if it made sense that someone consuming this content would potentially go on to become a customer or influence a customer of the business. In other words, did this content have any purpose for it?

The best blog post I've ever put on my personal website is a list of Harvey Specter quotes.[71] It crushes all of my other content tenfold, but it's completely useless to me or any business I might want to start. One small blog post that entertains or helps five key community members would be way more valuable than a viral post that 100,000 people see if most of the 100,000 have zero connection to your business.

I don't want you to think that every piece of content needs to deliver a specific return; that's not going to happen. But there needs to be some strategy behind the content you create. It needs to make sense that the content is going to help your community, build your brand, and ultimately lead to growth in your business.

---

[71] https://dannorris.me/harvey-specter-quotes/

By the way, it's perfectly valid to do it the other way, i.e., build an audience and then monetize it later. It's risky, but it can work as long as you have a strategy. You still need to build an audience who can ultimately buy or influence buying decisions in a community for your business offering. This is exactly what I did with my audience of income report readers who ultimately become WP Curve customers.

EXPERIMENT

I see great content marketers in the same way as I see great entrepreneurs. They aren't afraid to experiment until they find traction. It can be hard and possibly even embarrassing to try a lot of things and fail, but if that's what it takes to find something that works, then I say go for it. You might be surprised by what sticks.

Peter Thiel says, *"The paradox of teaching entrepreneurship is that such a formula necessarily cannot exist; because every innovation is new and unique, no authority can prescribe in concrete terms how to be innovative."*

The same can be said for content. When I first learned about content marketing, it was a rogue offshoot from blogging. Now, it's a normal part of life, and the richest and most successful among us are the ones who have been able to capture the most attention with their content. Today, Kim Kardashian is a billionaire, and I only had to write the first four letters of her surname; Google did the rest for me.

You can't profess to be an expert in this. The best content marketers commit to the experiment, they commit to innovating, and they search for and follow traction.

CONTENT MARKETING UNDER THE COMPOUND MARKETING MODEL

With all that theory in mind, let's get into some specifics.

Start with your communities. In our business, we have a whole range of different communities that are part of what we do. We have investors, homebrewers, local taproom customers, wholesale bars and restaurants, and bottleshops. We also have a whole bunch of people who are just following along with our journey. We have people who are interested in what we are doing from a business point of view.

Think about what different communities you have and what that means for your content. If you've defined a whole bunch of different communities, you can create content for each of them. Some might respond well to blog posts, some might love video, and some might only respond to in-person content.

You can break up your communities in many ways with different social media accounts, different brands, different sections on your blog, or different tags on your email list. But before breaking up these lists, make sure you think about your various communities and what they will respond to.

With that in mind, here are some marketing activities and general approaches to consider if you want to embrace Compound Marketing.

WEBSITE

Putting your website first in this list feels a little dated. Most attention these days is not on your website, but that doesn't mean it doesn't have a place. The website started as an online brochure, grew into a content hub, and is increasingly going back to being a brochure (depending on your industry).

Here are some pointers that I think always have and will always hold true:

- Whatever your website is, make it look good. Make it reflect the best aspects of your brand. More and more websites are going back to being the central representation of the brand, so they have to look good.

- I like to think your website can still be a content hub. Even if most of the attention for your brand is on social media, there is so much potential to build your site to be a hub for content. You can send people there for information instead of giving them a document, and you can use it for longer articles or help docs that can turn into guides or internal support policies. You could get super-transparent and use your website to post your business results, your policies, or your recipes. That all sounds aggressive, but I've done all of those things. Websites can be useful if they are interesting. People will go there if they are worth going to.

- Remember your communities. If you have a few very different groups of people, consider creating hubs on your site for each of these groups. Try to filter the right person into the right section so they are getting the content they need.

- One thing the website is still great for is getting signups for your email list. These days, you can get super-slick tools that will get signups with different tags in different sections, so you know what groups they are part of when they opt in. This is extremely powerful with email marketing. Whatever tools you use for this, make sure that when people opt in, you can tag them in some way so you know what they want.

Websites are still relevant, but unless they are content-producing machines, they are fast becoming the brochures of the pre-website era.

SOCIAL MEDIA

I don't want to talk too much about social media because I'll read this book five years from now and realize how wrong I was. That said, social media is the exact reason why websites aren't as important anymore. Attention has moved away from websites to the platforms that people are already on, day in and day out.

Even calling it "social media" feels a bit redundant.

That said, there are some universally good and universally bad ways to do social media. Here are some good ways:

- **Post the highest quality images** - It's important. It helps build the brand. Quality matters, and design matters. This is universal. It's always been true and always will be true. Quality matters.

- **Post customer stories** - If you can make your customer the hero of your story, take it. Every customer is an almost perfect replica of a potential customer. A hero customer is the best way to attract a potential customer. Tell their story.

- **Respond to and encourage comments** - Social media has proven to be an awesome way to engage a community and do it over time, and the best brands have built a giant following. Don't resort to bullshit conversation starters; that's a huge turnoff. Promote real questions and do the best job you can to engage with them. It takes a reasonable amount of effort for someone to ask a question in response to a post. It means a lot when you respond to it, and it also says something to them about their value when you don't.

- **Be as transparent and real as possible** - People love transparency. It's genuine and brings people into the story.

- **Share as much as possible, as often as possible** - Story features enable rapid-fire sharing, and the best brands are embracing it. Stay relevant, share lots of content, and ABTS (Always Be Telling a Story).

BRAND DESIGN

The brand is everything, so don't forget about its importance when it comes to Compound Marketing. With every piece of content you create, think about the brand. Put effort into designing it, and make sure it looks good. Great brands don't put out shitty looking content. They value it; they make it sexy.

ONLINE GROUPS

Getting a group together online can be extremely powerful and be an awesome content channel. Remember that groups are not just for your benefit; the members of the groups have lots of things they want to hear from you about. Online communities can be a great source of content ideas and a great place to get feedback on content.

With our Black Hops Ambassador group, we've found some posts in the group do better than our public posts. This is great because it means our members are fully engaged, and it doesn't take tens of thousands of followers to be recognized for some interesting piece of content.

MERCH

It's a bit of a stretch to call merch "content," but if you think about it, it kind of is. At least in our business, we've found merch to be an extremely powerful way to galvanize our communities, and the various messages we come up with are often best presented via merch.

Merch is one of the best storytelling tools because you can see people with the merch, and automatically, the story kicks off. That's especially true if you've done a good job with the merch offerings.

Here are some merch tips:

- Try as hard as you can as a general rule not to give away merch for free to just anyone. It under-values it and can get very expensive very quickly. A more targeted approach is needed.

- Given that last point, we should consider the power of giving merch away to the right people. Last week, I walked into a bottle shop owned by the biggest retailer in the country, and two out of the three staff members serving wore Black Hops t-shirts. That's pretty powerful!

- Merch is an awesome way to give you more excuses to post regularly and get the community (or communities) excited. Any new item is a great opportunity for a nice photo and more content, especially content with customers involved. Customers wearing merch is perfect Compound Marketing.

- If you have sub-communities within your group, consider merch for them. That's when things get really powerful. The smaller the group, the more passionate they are. If you have a small community within the main community, see what happens when you make merch just for them. We're about to launch our Black Hops Reserves shirts, and I suspect they are going to go very well.

There's a lot you can do with merch, and it can be hard at times to keep everyone happy, but it's worth the effort. People love physical things. No matter how online this world gets, that seems to be more relevant than ever.

BLOG POSTS/ARTICLES

Given my past, when I think of content marketing, I think of blog posts. I feel old even saying that, and the word "blog" has never appealed to me. In saying that, I think there is still a place for a well-written piece of content. Here are some helpers if you are doing written content:

- Write your posts for members of a specific community. At Black Hops, we might write a post for a homebrewer, we might write one for a venue owner, or we might write one on our story for a general follower of our business. But all of those are part of our communities, and we keep in mind who might want to read this post.

- Don't discount entertainment; reading is a hard slog. If you can be entertaining or you have people on board who can write in an entertaining way, get them involved. The more interesting, the better.

- Use your posts to tell a story. The written word is where you can really explore your story. It doesn't have to be super direct in the post, but anything you post about could be part of your overall story. For example, posts about business events could be part of your business story, posts about customers could be part of customer stories, and so on.

- Put the time in to make them as good as you can. I've learned this many times. I get excited about the act of publishing posts, but I am never excited about going back and changing them later. If you are really committed to giving as much value as you possibly can, you will put maximum time and effort into your posts. Agonize over every image, make it perfect, proof the words multiple times, structure it sensibly and visually well, choose a great featured image, pay attention to the font size and the contrast of font color and the overall size and feel of the page. How people feel matters a lot. You might not change this post much or ever in the future, but people will keep visiting it. Think about that. Steven Pressfield talks about the idea of resistance. It's a force that stops you from creating, and it gets you down.[72] Aim to overcome resistance, but at the same time, do great work. Quality matters. If you find this balance difficult, then welcome to one of the many challenges of business ownership and content creation.

Well-thought-out content on a website still has its place. The best way to make that happen is to make sure you create something good.

PODCAST

There is something very powerful about audio for people. It's intimate and real, and while the numbers might be low for a small business, the impact can be very high. I know that, in our business, there are a lot of people who've heard about us through the podcast, and I know our most-engaged community members listen to every episode.

It's hard to do a regular podcast; there's a fair bit involved. One thing I've found that helps is to do a podcast series based around new projects or new happenings within the business. This way, you can schedule a few episodes and lock it in and not feel like you have to do something every week. If you are down for doing it every week, that is better, and it's especially true if you can make it entertaining

---

[72] https://stevenpressfield.com/?s=resistance

and legitimately unique. There are so many podcasts now and so much competition that you have to bring something special. Any idea you have is probably worth exploring.

Podcasts are an awesome way to tell your story. If having your own podcast is too overwhelming, consider making a strong effort to go on other people's podcasts. It's a great way to get in front of new audiences, and it's a super-low commitment, plus, it's fun. Try to bring something unique to the show so you aren't just another guest.

NEWSLETTER

Email newsletters are still relevant. There are plenty of people who just want an occasional update on what you are up to. It's not the most personalized email marketing option, but it's a great reminder to update your audience, and it still has a place.

COMPETITIONS - EXTERNAL

Competitions provide a good free opportunity for some great content. In our industry, we have three major beer awards competitions each year, and we are also included in a few local business competitions. We've done well in these competitions, and it's served our business very well. The business competitions give us credibility as a business and also look good to our investors. It's not free, but it's normally pretty cheap to be involved, and depending on how valued the prize, it can be a real big win for your credibility. These are all great for the brand.

COMPETITIONS - INTERNAL

Doing your own competitions are equally powerful for exactly the same reasons, except it's your customers that are the heroes.

Your own competitions, particularly if they are merit-based, can be a great way to engage a specific audience. At Black Hops, we do an annual Black Hops Reserves brew-at-home competition where we give the members our recipes and get them to brew our beers and send them in for judging. It's an epic community builder, and it enables us to be transparent and get close to that segment of our community (homebrewers). We give the winners military-style pins and give coins for overall winners, which enables them to get discount beer and ultimate respect at our taprooms. We even have exclusive merch just for people who enter these competitions. This is a great way to engage your sub-communities.

PRESS

I've talked about the press plenty in this book already. There are pitfalls and downsides, and the constant regurgitation of the same story can be unpleasant. That said, I think getting press is almost always a good idea. We live in the age of attention, but I would never say to deliberately get bad press (bad press can be really shit). I would, however, say that press can be a really good brand builder. Plus, it's free! That makes it a great Compound Marketing strategy.

Get to know your local journalists and see where they are at with content. You might be working on content that could work for them. Journalists are like everyone else; they appreciate a bit of love. Make their job easier, give them some love, and don't be afraid to give them some ideas.

Just remember that they can turn on you. Things can go bad with journalists. You think you have a great relationship, and no matter the story, the relationship wins. Then when they kick the shit out of you, you realize that the story always wins. There's something noble about that, but just remember this if you are getting too close with a journalist.

SALES ACTIVATIONS

I hesitate to include this, but as someone with a physical product business, I can't ignore the value of having specific physical things in people's faces at the point of sale. It's extremely powerful and important and can't be ignored. It's also a great opportunity for more compounding:

- Use them to tell your story. Anyone who sees it is now interested long-term in what you're up to

- Make them look as good as possible. This is the best opportunity to showcase the brand

- Perhaps you can deliver some good content

Sales activations are a required part of what we do. Do your best to focus them on building the brand, not just flogging products, great images, unique design, promoting award wins, etc.

EVENTS/IN-PERSON

Events/in-person seems like an odd choice when we are talking about content marketing. Events feel like an old-school marketing initiative, but they can be so powerful, especially if you think about them within the Compound Marketing framework. If you believe that people care about brands and stories, what better way to promote this than via an event or in-person activity.

In our business, events are hard. Every event that comes up expects you to attend, takes most of your money, and assumes you will be happy at the end of it.

For the longest time, we just turned up and accepted the fate that you had to turn up at events and do your thing.

Since those days, we've found a better way to deal with events. Here are the criteria we use to determine if an event is useful or not, using the Compound Marketing model.

- Brand - Can we use this as an opportunity to showcase our brand? For us, it's cans of beer in people's hands and putting effort into our event stall. This is an in-person realization of everything we stand for. It's a chance for a new audience to see what we are about. It's a great opportunity for people to fall in love with a brand.

- Story - We use it to tell our story in person. Whether it be via the signage used, or the event collateral or the conversations with attendees, there's nothing more powerful than telling a story in person.

- Community - We look at how likely the event is to capture our key communities. For us, our local community is huge, and we've learned that local events are 100% worth investing in, but interstate events, not so much.

- Content - Depending on the event, they are also an opportunity to promote your content channels, especially social media. For example, we always see a huge amount of traction on social media as a result of us being at our local craft beer festival.

If we can get wins in brand, story, content, or community from an event, then it can be a great exercise. We aim for events to be a break-even activity. We focus them on building our most engaged communities and building our brand.

VIDEO

Video is a content medium that has exploded in recent years. To give you an idea, in 2019, users spent a weekly average of 6 hours and 48 minutes watching online videos. This was a 59% increase from just three years prior in 2016.[73]

These trends are continuing with every social media network focusing heavily on video. In years gone by, it was mainly YouTube but not anymore. TikTok is all video, Instagram now has inbuilt video, IGTV most stories are videos, and the new TikTok-inspired Reels is all video. Twitter and Facebook are also stacked with video.

Video can't be ignored anymore, and it's great for Compound Marketers because it's a great opportunity to showcase your brand and to make things real.

---

[73]   https://www.oberlo.com/blog/video-marketing-statistics

Keep video as high quality as you can, and use it as a way to get your audience really into what you are doing. There's nothing more real than video. Face-to-camera is great if you have someone who is keen to do that, and good at it, and highly produced video can also be great to build a brand. Poor video can do more harm than good.

LIVE

Live streaming has become a massive part of modern content platforms, and for the same reasons as video, it can be a great compounding channel. Live is as real and genuine as it gets, and if done well, it is an awesome way to engage your community.

We use live stream events via Zoom with some of our key audiences like our Ambassador Group for beer launches and tastings. We've used it when we are fitting out taprooms to show what we are working on and answer any questions, and also as a quick way to do a video and have it available on our social channels.

APPS

Apps are another channel worth considering. We have a local delivery app called Supply Drop that allows us to engage with people at a whole new level.

Having an actual app in the App Store is enough to get people committed to downloading it and having it on their phones. It opens up a new channel to engage them with notifications and gives you a place on their most important real estate (their phone screen). I wouldn't have an app for no reason, but if you can think of a good idea and use it to get more content to your people, an app is definitely worth considering. With modern no-code platforms, they can also be built pretty cheaply and quickly.

COMMUNITY-GENERATED CONTENT

Remember that what your audience wants to see doesn't necessarily have to come from you. If your community members are posting content, that could be just as powerful or even more powerful than your content.

Social media is a great example. You might as well share a great pic a customer has taken as opposed to your own professional photo. It will be more real, and it will help build the community. Online groups are another great example. It doesn't always have to be you posting the comments and questions; some of the best threads in our group are started by members. Once a community member can see that other people like them are really engaged in this community, it acts as social proof and will get them more involved. Sometimes, talking about yourself too much is a curse and having community members speak on your behalf is a lot more powerful.

When community members produce content, it's like they did your job for you. Embrace it.

More?

There are so many different options for creating content that they can't all be listed. The important part is always to hold up the quality of the brand, engage your communities with your content, and tell your story, regardless of the platform or medium.

CONCLUSION

JUSTIFYING YOUR MARKETING

I have an exercise that I do where I look at what we are doing with marketing, and I consider whether or not it's a compounding activity.

It may not be the right move to completely ignore all other options, but at least let this exercise be the thing that brings it to your attention and a decision point on whether you want to pursue it. Your mix of traditional vs. compounding might change over time.

The exercise is pretty basic, and it's based on this table:

Activity	Community	Strategy	Compound Marketing Justification

Under Activity, list the marketing activity you are spending time or money on. Under Community, list which one of your communities this serves. Remember, for any business, it's likely there are several communities your activities might serve. Under Strategy, write your strategy with this particular marketing activity. Under Compound Marketing Justification, list which one of the Compound Marketing platforms this activity is part of, e.g., brand, story, content, or community.

Let's say you have a local gym, and you market it in more traditional ways. Here are some examples of what you might do:

Activity	Community	Strategy	Justification
Google Ads targeted toward potential customers	Gym Members	Pay for specific keywords like '[location] gym'.	This will drive leads, but it won't compound and won't help you other than the immediate lead. It's also absurdly competitive and expensive because it's easy, obvious, and short-term in nature.
Local paper ads	Gym Members	Take out an ad, hope to get visits.	Won't compound. No justification.
Targeted Facebook ads	Members	Target people interested in workout accounts who are in a certain location.	Can be very effective but won't compound - only good for the immediate lead. Plus, you're relying on someone else's platform not your own.
Lock in memberships	Members	Force people to be locked in so they pay next month.	Creates resentment, hurts the brand, makes customers dislike you.
Sign out the front	Members	People who drive past will see the sign, maybe offer a special offer.	Might work, might also piss off current customers who won't get the offer. Won't compound.

You get the picture. These are traditional marketing activities that may or may not work in the short-term, but they certainly won't provide ongoing value. In most cases, they will also be expensive because most people are drawn to short-term fixes, and that makes them competitive and drives the price up.

Let's look at some compounding options, and you'll notice that a lot of these things are things that some of the best gym franchises and brands have been investing in over the last few years.

(If you want an easy Google Doc to download, you can grab the following at https://dannorris.me/resources.)

Category	Community	Activity	Justification
Website	Members and instructors and influencers	Make your website shit hot. Anyone who sees it will feel the value of the brand. It's a small and worthwhile investment. Use it to store great content, i.e., work out videos, competitions, challenges, recipes, expert interviews, member stories, etc. Build content hubs for your key communities.	Brand / Content / Community
Social Media			
Main social media platforms, posts, and stories	Members	Use your social media to tell stories of your members. Keep comments active, respond and engage with people, show behind the scenes things to get people deeper into the brand, share on the story as much as possible. Inspirational quotes can't hurt if your audience loves them.	Content / Story

Category	Community	Activity	Justification
Online groups	Members & instructors	You could use an online group like a Facebook group to engage members between visits. You could even do something like a Slack group for instructors to share notes. Make sure the groups are there for only the keenest members, keep it positive and legitimately engaging - no bullshit questions just for false activity.	Community
Merch	Members, instructors, influencers	There's nothing gym junkies like more than talking about how much they love going to the gym. Go hard on Merch. When they aren't at the gym they might as well be promoting the gym. And if you get paid for that to happen, it's an absolute no brainer. Have different options for different levels, i.e., instructors or challenge winners get exclusive merch that others can aim for. There are heaps that can be done with merch!	Brand / Community
Blog posts/ articles	Members, instructors, influencers	There's lots you can do here. Online workouts, member profiles, meal plans, diet/supporting content, online challenges, guest posts from instructors (good for them, good for you).	Content

Category	Community	Activity	Justification
Podcast	Members, instructors, influencers	Again the opportunities are endless here. Interviewing instructors or influencers, interviewing people with supporting content (health experts), showcasing members, etc.	Content
Newsletter	Members	As above, just another channel.	Content
Competitions	Members	Competitions are a great way to engage your community of members, and will also result in a whole bunch more content for you.	Community
Press	Members / Instructors	Look for press opportunities for members and instructors. A story about a gym probably isn't that exciting. A story about some great member results, or something interesting an instructor is doing, is much more interesting.	Community
Events	Members / Instructors	Lots can be done here, an in-person challenge, evening Q&A sessions with experts, higher-level seminars, monthly catch-ups, etc. Keep events focused on building the community.	Community

Category	Community	Activity	Justification
Video	Members / Instructors	Again, so much can be done here with video. Quick workout tips etc. What about some fun videos, or some inspirational non-conventional workout videos.	Content
Apps	Members	The best gyms have apps that are actually useful and that their members love.	Community

These are just really simple examples. I know nothing about gyms. I'm sure that whatever your business is that you can come up with some awesome ways to market the business using this method.

HOW TO MEASURE COMPOUND MARKETING

While giving up on ROI can put you in the right mindset for Compound Marketing, there is a downside. If you don't look at anything to determine if your efforts are having an impact, you could spend years doing a lot of work and getting no reward. Many people do, and in some cases, there is something to be said about putting in the often-referenced Malcolm Gladwell 10,000 hours required for mastery.[74]

That said, I think there are things you can look at to work out if your efforts are headed in the right direction. And there are certainly pitfalls when it comes to reporting on things like content and social media that will lead you astray. What follows are some useful guidelines.

---

[74]   https://en.wikipedia.org/wiki/Outliers_(book)

THE ULTIMATE MEASURE

The ultimate measure of how well your marketing is going is how well your business is performing. If your business is performing very well, in whatever metric that's important to you (your seats are full, or your monthly growth is as high as you'd like it, etc.), then your marketing, whatever it is, is enough.

It might sound like a pipedream to be in this situation, but I know a lot of entrepreneurs who are, and I've been there a few times as well. With WP Curve, 10% per month was as much growth as we could handle while we built a team to perform a pretty complex service 24/7 worldwide with no outside funding. At Black Hops, doubling every year is the maximum we could handle. In February last year, we had one brewery, 15 staff, 300 or so wholesale customers, 1 taproom, and were doing about 50,000 L per month. At the time of writing in June 2020, we have 2 breweries (the second one 10x the size of the first), 2 taprooms (about to open a 3rd), 31 staff, over 1,000 customers, and doing about 150,000 L per month.

It occurred to me today that, out of all the reports I get each week, month, quarter, and year, marketing is not one of them. We don't need more marketing, we don't need more out of our current marketing, and we don't need to hire any marketing people. Enough people are finding out about Black Hops and enough people care.

Not to say that marketing isn't important, and building these assets for the future isn't very much on my radar. The point is, the marketing we are doing right now is doing everything we need it to, and that's the only metric we really need.

That will probably change at some point, but it's important not to be distracted by things you don't need. If business is good, then you probably don't have a marketing problem.

USE YOUR INTUITION

Being the line-chart-loving, analytical person I am, it does pain me a bit to say this: Sometimes you just *know* when things are going well. We do brewery tours at Black Hops, and they are great. We don't give people a survey at the end, and we don't ask them for feedback. But we know they are good. We have a great story, a great facility, a great host, and we put a lot of effort into doing great tours. We can see people are happy in the end. They will buy merch and often leave reviews or share it on social media or just take photos as they go. That's enough. No more metrics are necessary.

When we do events, we don't do surveys about whether people liked our stall. We normally walk around and get a feel for how we are doing compared to others, have a beer at our stand, and see if it feels like it's going well. After a handful of events, we know when we do a good one and when we don't.

If you are producing loads of content and constantly having to promote it in Facebook groups and getting no traction, there's probably something wrong. You don't really need numbers to tell you that. Trying to measure something unnecessarily will be a big distraction and might even take the fun out of the whole thing.

AVOID VANITY METRICS

Vanity metrics have completely taken over modern marketing analytics, especially when it comes to social media. Metrics like total followers and total shares and reach and comments are literally driving people crazy.

Metrics like total followers or total likes are handy as a piece of social proof, but they aren't a good measure of how effective your content is, how much people care about your brand, or how engaged your audience is. They are a gigantic distraction, and focusing on those numbers will often lead you to focus on the wrong activity. Having 20,000 social media followers does you no good if those people don't care about you or they care about you for the wrong reasons.

Here are a few guidelines:

- On social media, look at shares and comments. Likes are very passive. If someone really cares about your content, they'll share it, and they'll comment. If you haven't had a post go well before, you'll know about it when it does; the traction looks very different.

- For long-form content like blog posts/articles, I do sometimes look at views, which isn't the best metric, but you can also take note of how it's being shared in various places. Similar to a social media post, if people are really into something, you'll see it turning up in other places.

- If the content or activity is directly associated with a product, then sales can be the ultimate metric. We regularly look at how quickly limited release beers sell out and what kind of traction they get on social media. This lets us know whether we nailed the product and the packaging and the social media content and story for that release.

- If you have a community like our Black Hops Ambassador Facebook group, look at how many discussions are happening in the group and not at how many members you have. Too many members can kill a great group. Once groups start regularly producing their own content without your intervention, you know you're winning.

ENGAGEMENT

Engagement is the best metric for any effort to provide content to a community. The goal is not to make your community bigger, but to make the members care more. If you make the members care more, they will grow the community for you, and you won't have to worry about attracting new members.

Some platforms will give you specific insights and tools for measuring engagement, but generally, the best way is to use your own intuition. Ignore the metrics they give you (like the number of followers and number of likes) and look for other indicators that things have hit the mark.

One of the best indicators of engagement is what people say in person. This has become obvious to me since starting a physical offline business using online marketing techniques. The best data I get for how things are going is what happens in person, especially for things we do online.

There is so much noise online that half of it needs to be ignored, and most of it can't be trusted. In-person, everyone dials it back to how they really think. I hardly ever hear about our podcast online; its metrics are not good. But in person, I've had hundreds of people tell me they listen to it and ask me about certain episodes and want to engage with me about the topics. This tells me it's meaningful.

When we launch a limited release beer, the taprooms get flooded with people coming in to buy it. If it's really good, they line up. If everything really hits the mark, they keep coming back to ask if it's back, they ring up and ask if we still have it, and they talk about it for months or, in some cases, years after we make it. Sometimes, if we do our marketing job too well, they are upset at us for not having the stock!

This information is priceless. This is when you know people are truly engaged with what you are doing, and no metric can give you this level of insight.

ENGAGE, DON'T TARGET

For the longest time, marketing has been looked at as an exercise in targeting people. What an awful metaphor. A person who's been targeted doesn't think higher of the assassin. We're in the business of building the value of a brand; that's what businesses do. That's what marketing goals should be tied to.

We don't want to line up our community members and target them. We want to engage them and make them love this brand and community even more. Targeting is and always has been an effective way to drive immediate sales, but it's not an effective way to build a brand.

The best brands engage their audience unlike anyone else. In doing so, they make them love the brand more. If done well, you should be able to reduce the amount of traditional marketing and reduce the amount of targeting. If done really well, you can eliminate it.

PATIENCE OVER PERSISTENCE

Entrepreneurs are always told never to give up. Persistence is a religious entrepreneurial commandment that is never questioned.

I've found persistence is not necessarily a good thing. Sure, hard work is a requirement for entrepreneurship, especially early on. But persistence gives the impression of continuing to do the same thing regardless of whether it's going well.

At times, I've stopped persisting. I stopped persisting when I gave up on my agency and analytics startup to focus on a new business (WP Curve). I stopped persisting when I sold WP Curve reasonably early into it and turned my attention to Black Hops. In hindsight, these were very good decisions.

I've done it many times with different types of content, different groups of customers, or different brands and angles for stories. If it's not working, persistence is the enemy. It kills opportunity because it forces you to focus on something that isn't working as opposed to something new and potentially great.

Patience, however, is a virtue. It is not the same thing as persistence. A compounding approach to anything requires patience. When you work on serving a group of people, and you work on building a brand and building stories and creating content, it takes time. That's because it requires you to build trust, and trust takes a long time to build. It's difficult, and it's not sexy to talk about because it most certainly will not result in you becoming a millionaire overnight.

Jeff Bezos recently said, *"You earn trust slowly over time by doing hard things well."*[75] Jeff operated Amazon unprofitably for ten years and barely profitable for another ten. But he built the most valuable company of our generation, and along the way, became the world's richest man. He built a company that has employed more people in the US in the last decade than any other company, and everyone there gets at least double the minimum wage.

---

[75]   https://www.rev.com/blog/transcripts/
jeff-bezos-opening-statement-transcript-antitrust-hearing-july-29

Amazon did not get to be the world's most valuable company by persisting with all of its ideas. On the contrary, it ran into a huge amount of major issues along the way, such as Apple crushing its CD business or Amazon itself crushing its own book sales business by innovating on electronic readers with the Kindle.[76]

Amazon's story is not one of persistence; it's one of patience. Under immense scrutiny, decade after decade, Jeff backed himself because he saw traction and believed in what he was doing. He built Amazon strategically and patiently.

This is the mentality required for Compound Marketing. Building brands takes a long time. Building a community that cares and content that gains eyes and ears takes a long time. There is no way around it.

DON'T LET COMPOUND MARKETING GO WRONG

The worst thing that could happen as a result of you reading this book is for you to use it as an excuse to fail.

For the longest time, marketing has been thought of as an activity. I went to university to learn how to do this activity and perform it for a company in return for a good income.

In most companies, this is still the model that exists. Marketing is seen as a job for someone, and as long as someone is doing their job, then the marketing box is ticked off. This model no longer works.

There's no point paying someone to undertake marketing tasks if you can get the right kind of attention without those tasks being performed. Those tasks may even do more harm than good.

Don't use this book as an excuse to tick off a list of marketing jobs that need to be done. That's not the point.

You can invest as much as you want in your brand, but if it's not a great business idea, it's wasted. I spent so much effort having a flawless payment processing gateway, yet it meant absolutely nothing.

You can tell whatever story you want, but if you can't back it up with a great product and a community who cares, it's useless.

---

[76] https://twitter.com/drose_999/status/1287944667414196225

You can have an awesome community who loves you but where no one wants to buy anything, and you have no business. This is the classic blogger's story: amazing blog posts with great support from their community of other bloggers but no business. Community is only one part of the equation.

And you can be the world's best person at pumping out content and still make no money. Content has the potential to be a giant distraction. If things aren't working, don't keep pumping it out. Failure is okay; move onto something else and rethink things. Unless you are a freelance journalist, you will never be paid based on how much content you produce. If you are a marketer, you will be savagely underpaid for most of your work and grossly overpaid for a tiny fraction of it. That's how it goes. As an entrepreneur or a business owner, you need to find that fraction. It might take a while.

HOW MUCH COMPOUND MARKETING IS THE RIGHT AMOUNT?

Compound Marketing is a long-term, asset-building strategy. When you make an investment in a compounding asset, you might get small returns in the short-term, but the bulk of the value comes from compounding over time. In a lot of cases, you have to sit it out for many years before you get a decent return. If your business needs leads right now, Compound Marketing is not going to generate them in the short-term. Most businesses will focus on short-term, non-compounding marketing strategies like paid ads and forget about compounding strategies.

You, as the business owner, have to decide what kind of mix is right for you. In my case, I abandoned any desire to focus on short-term strategies and went all-in with Compound Marketing. That resulted in many years of pain and failure, but it ended up also bringing me a lot of value in the long-term.

That is not necessarily the right approach for everyone. Perhaps there's a balance where you can do 30% immediate non-compounding strategies and 70% Compound Marketing activities to keep the business going in the short-term, but set it up for a competitively advantageous future.

This is an individual decision, but hopefully, after reading this book, you will see yourself making this distinction. You will know when you sign off on a suite of paid ads instead of a video series that you are actively choosing an option that will only give (potential) benefit in the short-term. It won't help you long-term. With that knowledge, maybe you will aim to do both, or maybe like me, you'll go all-in with Compound Marketing.

SCALING COMPOUND MARKETING

INVISIBLE COMPOUND MARKETING

When I wrote my second book, *Content Machine*, the biggest example of content marketing I could think of was Red Bull Stratos Space Jump.[77] Three years prior, Red Bull organized for Felix Baumgartner and Austrian SkyDiver to jump from space with a parachute and stream it live.

The idea took seven years to plan and execute, and when the jump took place, eight million people watched it live.[78]

The Stratos Space Jump was epic; you can't get much bigger than jumping out of space. It garnered a huge amount of attention, and it was supremely on brand and perfectly executed.

It's hard to think of a better content marketing example since.

Red Bull invested an estimated $30m in Stratos, and you'd have to think it would be more than that with all the years of planning and all the time spent.[79] There was Red Bull branding all over every

---

[77] https://www.redbull.com/int-en/projects/red-bull-stratos

[78] https://www.theguardian.com/media/2012/oct/15/felix-baumgartner-skydive-youtube#:~:text=A%20world%20away%20from%20the,million%20people%20live%20on%20YouTube.

[79] https://www.theaustralian.com.au/news/world/felix-baumgartners-plunge-from-stratosphere-breaks-broadcast-records/news-story/204e359cb84e66cc215b9fce5b28f074

piece of the footage. It was content marketing for sure and not just pure advertising, but it was a very obvious marketing effort. Some might say it was a stunt.

Last week, SpaceX launched their first astronaut into space in partnership with NASA, and it was viewed by more than ten million people live.[80] This wasn't a marketing exercise; it's just what you do when you send a rocket into space. Over six hundred million people watched the Apollo 11 moon landing in 1969.[81] SpaceX has live-streamed all of its launches, and they always get an enormous amount of attention.

This isn't marketing for SpaceX; it's just the normal course of operating their business. It doesn't look like marketing; no one sees it as marketing; it's purely organic and integrated into the normal daily work of launching rockets. It's just part of the job.

SpaceX was famously started by an internet entrepreneur who flew to Russia to buy a rocket and was unimpressed with the price, so he decided to make them himself.[82] This guy was talking about making a vegetable garden on Mars in 2001.[83] It's 2020 now, and last week, Elon's company became the only private company to ever launch humans into space. The company is valued at $36b.

At the same time, Elon has amassed an enormous following and therefore engaged an enormous community. At thirty-seven million twitter followers at the time of writing this, he has been accurately described as the first and only entrepreneur influencer.[84]

Do you think SpaceX spends much on marketing? This is an incredible story, with a gigantic community, a great brand, and exceptionally compelling content. They don't need marketing. The world watches when they operate their business as normal. Their customers are national space agencies like NASA, commercial satellite

---

[80]   https://www.space.com/nasa-spacex-astronaut-launch-viewer-record.html

[81]   https://www.space.com/16758-apollo-11-first-moon-landing.html

[82]   https://en.wikipedia.org/wiki/SpaceX

[83]   https://www.wired.com/2012/10/ff-elon-musk-qa/

[84]   https://awario.com/blog/tesla-on-social-media-the-chaotic-force-of-elon-musk/

operators, and governments around the world. Do you think their customers aren't watching these launches?

Maybe one day, when they colonize Mars, they will have normal folks like you and me as customers. I know we are watching, and they won't have to do any marketing to get our attention.

If content marketing is releasing something interesting that grabs attention for a business and builds trust, then SpaceX launches are the epitome of content marketing.

If Compound Marketing is "putting marketing effort on things that go up in value," then SpaceX launches are certainly that. What started as a crazy idea to grow veggies on Mars has turned into a brand that some people think is more likely than anyone else to save humanity from itself.

These examples are daunting. I know we can't all build rockets and colonize Mars, but I used to think that about the Red Bull Stratos Space Jump. And I used that to open my mind about what's possible with content marketing. Now, I look at that as more of a traditional paid marketing initiative, and I gain inspiration from more organic storytelling-based content like the SpaceX example.

You might be surprised; there might be something that you are doing anyway that is very interesting to people in your community. I've noticed this more and more in the beer game because our community is super into everything we do. But it never struck me before that the best marketing might be just doing exactly what you are already doing, only making sure you capture it well, deliver it on the right platform, and cultivate the community who loves it.

And if what you are doing is not that interesting, then you also have the option of doing something else. Would you rather spend 50% of your time working on your business, and 50% of your time pushing hard to market your business to try to make it interesting, or 100% of your time on an interesting business and 0% on marketing? I choose the latter.

For some companies, marketing is not an activity anymore; it's just part of business. The right kind of attention is what matters, and if you can get it without any kind of marketing, then that's perfect.

DOES COMPOUND MARKETING SCALE?

From my first blog post in 2010 until the time of writing this in 2020, I've regularly had the same objection toward this approach to marketing. It doesn't scale.

While it's easy for a solo web developer to write some blog posts and generate some leads, there comes a point where companies need to spend money on marketing, and these organic approaches don't work. The 7.5% marketing spend comes into play.

My first business was a six-figure web agency business where I worked mainly by myself and with a few contractors. We turned over around $100,000/year or $8,300/month. 7.5% would have been $600/month, which was about what I spent on marketing.

My second business, WP Curve, was a seven-figure business. It turned over around $1,000,000 a year or $83,000/month. If we had to pay what the average company paid for marketing, we would have had to pay over $6,000/month. We didn't, though. We didn't spend much on marketing at all, and that $6,000/month went into a healthy profit for the founders. But still, the question plagued me about whether this approach could continue scaling.

This month, my current business, Black Hops, has done over $1,000,000 and will do over eight figures or $10,000,000 this financial year. If we had to pay what the average consumer goods company paid in marketing (actually 10.9%, not 7.5%), we would have to spend over $100,000 per month on marketing. That's well over a million dollars every year. We spend 1% to 2% on marketing, often under 1% in any given month. And this business has doubled every year since we started it, making it one of Australia's fastest-growing companies.

But there are much bigger companies than mine who have grown in the same way. Joe Rogan has never advertised his podcast, but he recently signed a licensing deal with Spotify rumored to be worth over $100m. And that's just for the privilege of playing his podcast episodes. How much is the whole thing worth if just the right to play the episodes is worth north of a hundred million dollars? Five hundred million? A billion? All grown organically.

Tesla does not spend any money on advertising.[85] They compete with the likes of Ford, who spend north of $4b per year.[86] Tesla just became the single most valuable carmaker in the world, with a market cap of $190b. Ford is tenth.[87] Tesla is valued higher than Ford, General Motors, Honda, and Fiat Chrysler put together.[88]

Tell me that investing in your story and your brand doesn't work at scale.

---

[85] https://minutes.co/3-ways-tesla-out-marketed-ever
y-other-car-company-in-2019-spending-0-on-advertising/

[86] https://mediakix.com/blog/tesla-advertising-zero-spend-budget-charts/

[87] https://www.rushlane.com/top-25-most-valuable-car-brands-2020-12364681.html

[88] https://www.forbes.com/sites/johnkoetsier/2020/06/11/why-tesla--gm--honda-
-ford--fiat-chrysler--daimler/#39334e4e20d1

A NEW KIND OF
ENTREPRENEUR

When I first started out in business, I had my own idea about what an entrepreneur was. A typical sales guy who had the gift of the gab, wore a neat, pin-striped suit, and drove a BMW sedan. Whether I was right at the time, I'm not sure, but that's certainly not the only option for an entrepreneur these days. We come in all shapes and sizes, which is great for people like you and me who don't fit that typical mold.

As an entrepreneur, you are probably going to work a lot, and you have to do something with your time. I know many business people, and they all approach this in very different ways. I know people who do wear suits and spend all day in meetings with people closing deals. I know others who study every bit of theory and apply every speck of it to their business. I know others who work deep in the business as the main go-to person for a whole range of jobs.

And then there are people who I think take a fairly new approach. They aren't necessarily the person hustling every sale, and they aren't winning the meeting lottery. They're focusing on the intangible things that they have faith will grow their business long-term, things like brand, story, content, and community. I used to feel guilty working on these things, but after building a six-figure, seven-figure, and eight-figure business, and seeing other entrepreneurs building nine, ten figures, and beyond, I no longer have that same feeling of guilt.

My call-to-action for you after reading this book is this: Be this new kind of entrepreneur, at least be more of this kind of entrepreneur than you were before reading the book. Take a leap of faith; invest in things that will result in your business building itself down the track as opposed to things that will only increase revenue right now. Never stop valuing your brand. Cultivate your story and chase better stories. Work out your core communities and invest in giving these people the best content in the world for free. Do it so much it feels uncomfortable, and do it long enough to get the benefit of that compounding over time.

Printed in Great Britain
by Amazon

51163080R00090